Oonagh O'Brien & Julie Kavanagh

A RESOURCEBOOK FOR
Parish Leadership Groups

the columba press

First published in 2001 by
the columba press
55A Spruce Avenue, Stillorgan Industrial Park, Blackrock, Co Dublin

Cover by Bill Bolger
Origination by The Columba Press
Printed in Ireland by Colour Books Ltd, Dublin

ISBN 1 85607 317 3

Acknowledgements

Foremost we would like to acknowledge the contribution made to this book by the people – laity, religious and priests – of the diocese who make up the leadership groups in the parishes of the Dublin Archdiocese. Their experience is expressed through these reflections and resources.

We also acknowledge the help and support of co-ordinators for Parish Development and Renewal, past and present. In particular we thank Micheal Comer, Eilis 0'Malley, Brid Liston, Jane Ferguson, John McSweeney, Breffni McGuinness and Grainne Doherty.

Special thanks to Donal Harrington and Majella Murphy for advice and editing, and to Mary Dent in the Parish Development and Renewal office for all her help.

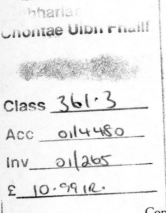

Contents

Foreword

Reflection on leadership within the Christian community today takes place in the context of changing leadership styles in the world around us. It is impossible to avoid being influenced by models of leadership in other cultures and in the secular world. This can be for our good. One Oriental writer ponders on effective leadership in this way: As for the best leaders, the people do not notice their existence. The next best, the people honour and praise. The next, the people fear, and the next the people hate. When the best leader's work is done the people say, we did it ourselves (Laotzu). Experience teaches us that where people are involved in making decisions that effect their lives they are much more likely to get involved when it comes to implementing those decisions. Engagement in and a deepening sense of responsibility for the parish do motivate people to greater commitment.

In inviting people to engage more fully in the life of their parish there is a gospel principle at stake. What is done together in unity is more fruitful for the spread of the gospel than any lone ranger apostolate. Unity in charity is the gospel lived and that lived unity makes the gospel attractive. It is helpful to remember that charity is first of all a gift of God before it is an obligation to live in particular ways. The task of leadership is to lead people to where they are most receptive to this gift and most free to respond to it.

With the emergence of leadership teams in more and more parishes there is an urgency about providing supports for them so that they can be as effective as possible in their ministry. As leaders they seek to help parishioners become more authentic in their living of the gospel and more consciously missionary in what they undertake. The starting point for effective leadership of this kind is reflective living, pondering in a prayerful way on what God is giving and asking at this time. A key task for leadership is that of reading the signs of the times in faith and deciding how best to respond to them. This is taking responsibility at the deepest level for the quality of parish life. It recognises how each person is uniquely blessed with gifts and limitations. Enabling giftedness and limitations to work well for the good the whole community requires wisdom and skill. The leadership team has to keep its eyes on the bigger screen and discern how the different talents of individuals can be channelled so that they work in harmony for the good of the whole people.

In the pages which follow, a wide range of resources is provided for these leadership groups. The team needs resources for the formation for its own members, it needs accumulated wisdom to guide its decisions, it needs skill so that it can reflect in prayer and discern accurately what God is saying through the events of this time. It will find a wealth of material on those and other topics in this volume. Because it meets a felt need, this volume, like the earlier volumes from Parish Development and Renewal, is sure of a warm welcome.

Bishop Martin Drennan
(Chair of Committee for Parish Development and Renewal)

Introduction

The process of Parish Development and Renewal in the Dublin Diocese has been ongoing over the last fifteen years. During that time many parishes have become involved in thinking of, praying for, planning and initiating renewal in their parishes. The work of Parish Development and Renewal over these years has been to support, resource and walk with these parishes as they make the process their own for their own situation. Much has already been written and published about the origins and development of the process as well as the resources produced along the way. In this latest volume we hope to pick up on some of the current themes emerging in parishes and to present some new resources to supplement those already published.[1]

KEY INSIGHTS REGARDING THE PROCESS OF RENEWAL IN ACTION

In presenting this volume we believe that it reflects some new key insights on the process of Parish Development and Renewal. We anticipate that the following eight insights will be seen by the reader to permeate this book. These insights lie behind both the content and the path that this resource book will take. In summary they are:

• Sharing leadership begins with the fulltime parish team.

• Parishes need leadership.

• The leadership group has a particular role within the parish.

• The leadership group is different from others groups in the parish.

• The necessity of reflective practice.

• The need to understand what happens in groups.

• The importance of saying what we are about.

• The need to focus on mission.

---

1. *Parish Renewal* (2 Vols), Donal Harrington, Columba Press, 1997
Prayer for Parish Groups, Donal Harrington and Julie Kavanagh, Columba Press, 1998

Sharing leadership begins with the full time parish team

The first key insight from the Parish Development and Renewal process is that collaboration, co-responsibility and shared leadership begin with the present fulltime team. It is initially the invitation from the parish priest that enables collaboration to happen. Two consequences follow from this:

- It is increasingly recognised that the parish priests' collaboration must begin with the team of fulltime pastoral workers in the parish, be they curates, vowed religious or fulltime lay people. A parish priest who espouses collaboration and shared leadership with parishioners but not with his fellow fulltime workers in the parish raises many questions. Parish Development and Renewal has and does work where there is a lack of involvement of curates or of the parish priest, but ultimately it is open to real difficulties.

- It is important that together with the parish priest, the fulltime team discusses, discerns and develops a sense of what is meant by collaboration and involving lay parishioners in leadership in the parish.

Parishes need leadership

A second insight gained in recent years is that now more than ever parishes need leadership. The leaders needed for our parishes today will embrace change and will have to be able to live happily with constantly unfamiliar situations. Furthermore, this will take place at a time when the numbers of traditional parish leaders, i.e. priests, are dropping and at a time of unprecedented social change in our country, which has brought with it a change in our experience of church.

The work of a leadership group supplements the role of the ordained priests. It does not overtake their role nor does it change the role of lay people. Rather it expresses the fulfilment of both roles. Sharing leadership is not only expedient in present circumstances; it is what we are meant to be about.

The Leadership Group has a particular role within the parish.

A third key insight is the emergence of the recognition that the core group/pastoral council/leadership group in the parish needs to pay increasing attention to its role as the parish group charged with keeping in mind the overall picture of the parish. Because of this we are deliberately using the term *leadership group* for the title and content of this book. We do this for two reasons.

First, in parishes there are many different names used for the group that takes overall care of the parish. These include core group, council, forum, team, co-ordinating group. Core group is the one most associated with the Parish Development and Renewal process but this is changing. In an effort to include all the aforementioned groups, and others, we have chosen a descriptive term rather than a title.

Second, we believe that 'leadership group' best describes the present reality in parishes as well as the future challenges. To describe a group as being in leadership in the parish is an expression of the belief that co-responsibility and, more importantly, collaboration are grounding principles of the Christian life. To be Christian is to be collaborative. This collaboration takes many forms and one of those forms is shared parish leadership.

The Leadership Group is different from other parish groups

This leads to a fourth emerging insight. There is a difference between other groups in the parish and the leadership group. Involving parishioners in the leadership group needs special consideration. For this central group the level and understanding of involvement is key. 'Involvement', in this case, is not just in any parish ministry but is specifically in the ministry of think-ing, praying, visioning and planning, along with the fulltime parish team, for the overall renewal of the parish. This is not to suggest that other groups operating in the parish are not or do not have to be collaborative, prayerful and planning.

The necessity of reflective practice

A fifth key insight is the necessity for reflective practice. There are two ele-ments to this. One is our increasing understanding of the centrality of prayer to the process of Parish Development and Renewal. It is clear, from our experience, that those groups who make prayer an integral part of meetings and who focus prayer on the work in hand, are the ones who seem to stay together and to be most focused.

A second element of reflective practice is the emerging need for time to reflect, discern and plan. Any one who has ever been part of a group or committee knows that for some people the vision and purpose of a proposed action are the most important matters to discuss. For others, getting on with the action and getting the job done are central. As leadership groups have developed in parishes we have seen an increased need for this central group to be as reflective as it is active. As the group charged with the overall view of the parish, the umbrella or helicopter group (as the group is sometimes described) needs to employ a good balance between action and reflection.

The need to know what happens in groups

A sixth key insight is that leadership groups working in the parish benefit from having some understanding of what is happening in the group, as a group. Some understanding of the people they are working with, how decisions are made, how the group is best organised so that members' gifts are shown and utilised, and how to deal with conflict, are all areas that emerge regularly for groups. When these issues are not dealt with they will often emerge as the question 'how can we work well together?'

The importance of saying what we are about

A seventh insight is the need for a group to have an articulated understanding of what it is about. The question 'what should we be about?' or 'what is the purpose of this group?' is often asked. And it is a very important question. A solid grounding in a sense and vision of church and parish, an appreciation and opportunity to discuss and discern the current situation in one's own parish, and time and energy spent developing a mission statement, are all necessary.

The need to focus on mission

Finally, the eighth key insight is that leadership groups need to be focused on mission. The distinction between a concentration on maintenance rather than mission cannot be overstated. A parish concentrating on maintenance may well be a very busy, active parish. There is so much to be done to simply provide a service and plan from one event to the next. A concentration on mission, on the other hand, acknowledges that because there is much to be done, we need to focus and plan. A missionary outlook for the parish takes the view that the broader picture must be attended to and that we need to see the parish as a place of ministry, belonging and community. In working towards the wider picture and in planning for the future, we trust that what *needs* to get done is more likely to get done.

HOW TO USE THIS RESOURCEBOOK

This resourcebook contains a substantial number of resources. It would be both impossible and unwise to expect any individual or group to work through these resources from beginning to end, one by one. This resourcebook is a tool and, as in the case of any tool, the level of value gained by its use will depend on how appropriately it is used.

A few starting points might help you to make the most of this book. They are as follows:

- We envisage that this resourcebook will benefit a number of different groups. These include those in fulltime parish leadership (i.e. the parish priest, curate, vowed religious sister/brother, pastoral worker), an already established parish leadership group, and a parish leadership group in formation.

- Our hope is that, prior to working with a parish leadership group, the fulltime parish team will do some initial thinking and reflection by themselves, using this resource material. We would encourage the fulltime parish team to work through the first four sections of this book together at an early stage. Indeed many of the resources found in section four are geared towards the fulltime parish team rather than a leadership group. (See the resourcebook overview below.)

- Even when a parish leadership group is established, we hope that the fulltime parish team would continue to draw on this resource material for on-going formation, especially when this team experiences change in its membership.

- We cannot overstate the wisdom of planning a leadership group's formation. Considerable thought needs to go into what path this formation will follow – and this path will vary from situation to situation. This resourcebook is intended to offer resources to meet the needs of those facilitating the initial and on-going formation of parish leadership groups. An early question to ask, then, is *who will be responsible for planning this path of formation?*

- Those responsible for planning the path of formation might be served well by asking themselves a number of questions, with this resource-book in hand. What areas does the group need to explore at this stage of its existence? What resources meet these needs? In what order will we explore them? When? What time do they need and what time can we give? What preparation needs to be done before using particular resource material? What resources will we explore at a later date? When? How will we help ensure that the leadership group receives on-going formation? How do we help ensure that this on-going formation meets the real needs of the parish leadership group?

- The resources within this resourcebook vary in their nature. Some are written reflections intended to offer information and insights and to stimulate discussion; to this end they will be followed by reflection questions. Some are active exercises; they will contain a step-by-step guide for carrying out the exercise. Some are aids to prayer, to help members reflect on particular issues; again these will have clear directions as to their use.

- Both those overseeing the formation of the leadership group and the leadership group itself will find it helpful to use an outside facilitator when working with some of these resources. This is particularly true of resources that are activity based or that deal with the identity of the group itself and its planning for the future. When dealing with these issues every member of the group needs to be able to fully participate and interact with the resource material. So a further question to ask in choosing to use particular resources is: Do we need an outside facilitator? (In the Dublin Diocese, the co-ordinators for Parish Development and Renewal are available to parishes to carry out such facilitation work.)

- We would recommend that every member of the fulltime parish team and the parish leadership group have a copy of this resourcebook. This gives everyone the opportunity to do outside reading and reflection in their own time and, importantly, it gives an equality of access to information.

- We begin each section of the resourcebook with its own introduction. This introduction gives an indication of the resource material that will follow and helps to put it in context. It will sometimes offer suggestions as to how best to use the resources that follow. At other times it may refer back to previous material, if appropriate. It is important, therefore, to read these introductions.

- These resources are not intended to be exhaustive. The last word in parish renewal and parish leadership groups has not been written! We hope that the resources in this resourcebook touch into and help explore the central issues for today. Of course, there are other resources available that we hope groups will draw upon in conjunction with these particular resources.

A RESOURCEBOOK OVERVIEW

This resourcebook follows a definite path from beginning to end. As we have said previously, we see a value in the fulltime parish team working through the first four sections together before returning to section one and what follows with a parish leadership group.

To make sense of this suggestion, and to further help the users of this resourcebook to make best use of it, it may help to give a brief overview of the path we have taken:

It is important to place any discussion of parish and renewal in the context of the world and, more specifically, the country, we live in today. We begin this resourcebook with the premise that to understand parish renewal we need to take account of: *The context for Parish Renewal today* (Section 1), and *The nature of Parish Renewal* (Section 2).

It is out of the above context and understanding that a parish leadership group will operate. But you will want to know what we mean when we talk about a parish leadership group and what we think a parish leadership group should be about. Hence our next step on the journey is: *'What should a parish leadership group be about?'* (Section 3)

Knowing what a parish leadership group should be about is not enough, however. The existence of a parish leadership group within a parish brings with it very specific demands and challenges for those already working full-time in the parish. We grow ever stronger in the opinion that these people within the parish need to give time to exploring the implications for themselves, their expectations around a parish leadership group and their tangible support for it. To help such exploration we provide a set of resources in: *Getting ready for a parish leadership group.* (Section 4)

The next step is to bring on board members of an existing or an establishing parish leadership group. This requires, as we have said above, the need to plan for their initial and on-going formation. Obviously many of the resources in the first four sections will be of value to the group. We recommend that those planning the formation need to look back at these sections and draw appropriately from them; they can then move forward into the following sections of the resourcebook. In the early stages of a group's formation we hope that time will be given to getting to know one another and to begin to name the variety of gifts within the group. It is these same gifts that the group will draw upon to accomplish its work together. The above recommendations are made clear in the introduction to: *Coming together as a Parish Leadership Group.* (Section 5)

At the heart of our vision and understanding of parish renewal is an attitude of collaboration – an attitude that sees every member of the parish as having the potential to contribute to some degree to the life of the parish. To help tease out this foundational understanding further we offer: *Collaboration: The 'how' of a Living Parish.* (Section 6)

Out of this collaborative stance to parish members comes a particular understanding of collaborative parish leadership, explored in: *Collaborative Parish Leadership.* (Section 7)

But collaboration is more than mindset and understanding. It will bear fruit in activity and in how we go about that activity, with an eye to the future. Because we are engaged in relationship with one another it will also bring with it the practical struggles and issues that arise in working together. Resources for carrying out these practical activities and exploring the issues that arise in working together are provided in: *Collaboration: Some Tools for the Task.* (Section 8)

Any of the work we do together, in the Christian context, does not make sense apart from a spirit of prayer. Prayer should guide the choices a group makes, the directions its follows, its sense of who the group are. In light of this belief, we have devoted an entire section of this resourcebook to prayer – specifically to why and how a group might go about making prayer a key part of its time together. Practical resources and examples are given to help members of the parish leadership group take responsibility for leading prayer at its meetings in: *Prayer – the 'why' of a Living Parish*. (Section 9)

Throughout this resourcebook we hope that readers will pick up a sense of the importance of the parish leadership group looking beyond itself. While many of these resources are concerned with the group and with helping the group grow, this is always with the purpose of helping it to fulfil its role within the parish to the best of its ability. The parish leadership group is, at its core, helping to serve in a particular way the mission of the church – to build up the Body of Christ. Its ultimate direction of concern then is outward – to the rest of the Body of Christ. The parish leadership group is never intended to be an inward-looking, self-absorbed group. Rather, it is called to embrace the missionary mandate of all the members of the church. This handbook, then, ends by exploring this pivotal notion in: *Mission – Sustaining Parish Renewal*. (Section 10)

SECTION ONE

The Context for Parish Renewal Today

Introduction

In this section we will focus on the context for renewal today and therefore the context in which a leadership group in a parish operates. It is not our intention to give lengthy reflections on the theology of parish or a social critique, but rather to provide some brief ideas to be of use, we hope, in your own thinking and discussion.

It is important for you, as either members of the fulltime parish team or members of the parish leadership group, to have a sense of the great change and new challenges facing parish life today. The following passages are offered as resources for reflection and discussion. They address the context of society today, in which a leadership group has to carry out its work.

For optimum use of the material, we suggest that you begin with the exercise in resource 1.1. After that you might choose to take resource 1.2, 1.3 and 1.4 together or separately as a basis for discussion. Reflection questions for these three resources are given at the end of resource 1.4. These questions might help to foster discussion among the group on the context of parish in Ireland today.

RESOURCE I.I PARISH TODAY

This resource will help members to reflect on their own experience of parish and to begin to look to the future. Again this resource is intended as a gentle introduction to the following resources in this section.

Begin by taking some time together as a group to discuss the following questions:

- With regard to parish life what are some of the biggest changes that have taken place during your lifetime?
- What do you see as the greatest challenges facing your parish today?

RESOURCE 1.2 OUR SENSE OF CHURCH: A REFLECTION

Parish has been and remains the place of gathering and growth for baptised people. The parish remains the place where the majority of people experience church. While it can be argued that the site of community is moving from parish or is disappearing altogether, it is at parish level that most people continue to come in contact with the Christian community.

There are many challenges and opportunities facing parishes today, both internal and external. There is a sense that the challenge facing parish renewal today is not people's sense of spirituality but rather their sense of church. At a time in this country when renewal has become a real focus for the church, we find ourselves increasingly part of a society that is moving away from the church. This is part of the reality of parish renewal today. We are not unique in this trend. It is being experienced in many other countries around the world, particularly in the western world.

We also hear very often today that people, especially the young, will say that they are interested in spirituality but not in religion. There is a definite move away from the institutional and hierarchical church but openness to spirituality. We are left with the question: how do we, at parish level, respond to this interest amongst young people?

There is also much confusion, hurt and a feeling of helplessness about the many scandals that have rocked the church. For those of us involved in parish renewal, we believe it is important to acknowledge and be able to discuss what is happening around us. We are none of us immune to the current climate of secularism or to the huge challenges facing the church internally.

RESOURCE I.3 IRELAND TODAY: A REFLECTION

The following are some ideas and opinions about our society today.

We live in a country where we are increasingly told that what you do, how much money you earn, where you live and what you wear, are of vital importance. People can feel judged in terms of efficiency, productivity and achievement output. The 'worth' of a person seems more and more to lie in his/her capacity to earn rather than in any inherent value. Many experience that ours has become a disposable, throwaway society with a focus on the outer characteristics of things and ultimately people, rather than on inner value.

In our country today there is much more freedom, transparency and prosperity. Although painful at times, there is a feeling that past wrongs are being exposed and dealt with. People feel less dominated by church and state and the movement towards individualism has brought about a greater respect for the dignity and uniqueness of all human beings.

Throughout Western Europe and the United States, consequent upon the gradual breakdown of 'traditional' culture, there is a real experienced crisis of meaning. Formerly people lived life as though in an objectively ordered universe where values and meaning were 'independent' of the person. The emphasis was on conformity, and order was ascribed to a divine source.

There has been unprecedented economic development in our country in the last decade. One of the consequences of economic growth is that people become more individualised, with an emphasis on personal autonomy and the development of individual belief and value systems. This process, as well as people's reactions to church scandals, has meant a significant decrease in participation in parishes.

RESOURCE 1.4 FORWARD WITH CONFIDENCE

The following passage gives a particular view for Christians in Ireland today.

'It is our conviction that the Christian message retains all its potential to enable people in Ireland to meet the novel challenges and opportunities of economic wealth in an authentically human way. We say this despite abuses that have been perpetrated by some trusted representatives of the church. But while we wrestle with the implications of those shameful events, and the legacy of an Ireland in which people who were poor had few, if any, rights acknowledged, we know that the strength and power of the Christian gospel are not, ultimately, dependent on weak human beings. Confidence in the gospel, therefore, rather than in ourselves, brings us to hope ...' *(Prosperity with a Purpose,* 1999)

REFLECTION QUESTIONS FOR 1.2, 1.3, 1.4

From what you have read and in light of your own experience:

How do you think people view 'parish' today?

How do you think people view themselves in relation to 'parish' and in relation to 'society' today?

What do you think is the central message in the passage from *Prosperity with a Purpose?*

SECTION TWO

What is Parish Renewal?

Introduction

The following resources can be used as background reading for a leadership group. Members might choose to read the material (2.1 and 2.2) at home and discuss it when they come together. Enough time should be given in a discussion for members to tease out their own reactions to and comments on the material.

RESOURCE 2.1 RENEWAL TODAY

A great effort is needed by priests and laity to renew parish life in the image of the church herself as a communion benefiting from the complementary gifts and charisms of all her members. Communion is a dynamic reality, which implies a constant exchange of gifts and services between all the members of the people of God. The vitality of a parish depends on merging the diverse vocations and gifts of its members into a unity which manifests the communion of each one and of all together with God the Father through Christ, constantly renewed by the Grace of the Holy Spirit. *(Pope John Paul II in an address to the American bishops)*

Renewal is one of those words with which we can easily become over familiar. There is therefore the danger that we can lose a shared understanding of what renewal is about. At parish level, renewal has both a very broad and a very specific meaning. In the broad sense, we are all called to constant renewal in our personal and collective journey to God. For the baptised, the parish, as the site of holiness, is the setting and context within which this continual conversion takes place. Each Sunday we reaffirm this commitment to our life in Christ as we listen to our story in the readings and share eucharist, the very essence of our life in Christ. And each year we make a specific recommitment when we renew our baptismal promises at the Easter vigil.

In the more specific sense, as parish community we are constantly called to renew the life of the community in light of church teaching and in response to current pastoral needs.

The 'new' understanding of parish includes the call to respond to the current 'signs of the times', to discern where the Spirit is moving us in our particular context, in our particular time. This is partly why renewal is best understood as a process rather than a programme.

For a leadership group the task of renewal is both broad and specific:

- In broad terms it is to support the journey to holiness of all parishioners.
- In specific terms it is to attend to the present needs, pastoral concerns and future directions in the particular parish.

Because of the variety of pastoral needs to be responded to, renewal can look very different in each parish. However, we believe that there are two central characteristics which are signposts of renewal.

Characteristic 1: Relationships

The need for relationship is very basic for every human being. In isolation, without relationships, we would find it very hard to survive. As humans we are social beings who are sustained by a network of familial and social relationships. In this context, a parish is a social construct of many and varied relationships.

Renewal of parish is about people, and therefore is about relationships: how we relate to ourselves, to God and to other people. In the broad sense, the quality of renewal in a parish will be mirrored in the quality of relationships within that parish.

As a religion Christianity is firmly based on relationship. The Trinitarian relationship of the love of Father, Son and Holy Spirit, tells us of the mystery of communion, love and fidelity at the heart of the Godhead.

One of the defining characteristics of parish renewal in the Dublin Diocese over the past fifteen years has been the quality of the relationships amongst people involved in renewal. As the experience of renewal has grown and developed in parishes, it has become clear that a concern for the group as a 'team' has been central to success. This includes a concern to get to know one another and to know how to work well as a group.

A willingness to set aside time for a group to get to know each other, to socialise together, to pray and learn together, strengthens the sense of 'team'. There is no one formula for this. Openness and a willingness to learn are required. The focus of getting our relationships right is the building of community.

Characteristic 2: Community

Genuine communities are made up of people who are:

- Committed to one another
- Share a common vision or goal
- Have a sense of purpose
- Share a common meaning about what they are doing together.

In its essence, as seen in the gospels and the early church, Christianity offers a way of being with people. The unity of the church today is based on the community as one, as the body of Christ. Our parishes today are the models of this belief. They are both medium and message. Perhaps one of the most long-lasting and predominating features of parish is that it gives a structure, within which we can experience ourselves as Christian community. A focus on building community begets a sense of belonging, which begets participation.

The idea and ideals of community are deeply rooted in our Christian tradition. Community as a term and a phenomenon is also a recognised sociological reality.

So what is it that makes a Christian community? In *The Final Report of the Anglican-Roman Catholic International Commission* (1982) an excellent description of the term, based on the New Testament is given. In the New Testament the word *Koinonia* is used to describe community. This describes:

Firstly, the sharing relationship, or solidarity, of God with God's people – through our relationship with the Father (1 Jn 1:3), Son (1Cor 1:9), and Holy Spirit (2 Cor 13:14).

Secondly, it describes the partnership between Christians in the faith (Phil 1:5).

Thirdly, the word emphasises the identity and significance of those in fellowship as unique persons. (Gal 2:9)

Fourthly, Koinonia is used to describe the mystery of the eucharist. (1 Cor 10:14ff).

Fifthly, Koinonia is community not only as a sharing of relationship but of material goods. (Acts 2:44 and Rom 15:26)

We have already acknowledged that community is a sociological as well as a theological term. We are communitarian, not just because we are Christian, but because we are human. There are many challenges facing community today. People, particularly in urban areas, are finding it increasingly difficult to find and experience community. It is important to acknowledge that some people in our parishes do not experience parish as the site of community. However, it is equally important to acknowledge that this challenge to the local parish is similar to that facing community groups, voluntary organisations and other community oriented groups. The local parish increasingly needs to take its place among these other groups in its efforts to facilitate, support and sustain community.

To this end, the local parish should feel that it has the right to address issues relating to unemployment, drug abuse, suicide, isolation, refugees – if these are live issues facing its members. While recognising the statutory duty of government to respond to these issues, a local parish community cannot strive to be a real experience of community if it chooses to ignore basic life issues that are facing its members everyday.

Finally, we attempt to build and sustain community because of the belief that we are, by our nature, social and community-minded rather than simply individuals. We are all in need of support – the support of loving friendship, common prayer and challenge. This may seem a very obvious point but the basis of renewal is a willingness by individuals to become involved, to be open to creating and supporting a common vision and to communicate honestly and openly with one another.

Conclusion

If we take these two characteristics, relationships and community, as outlined above, then we will realise that renewal is a continual process, calling for ever-new responses. We never reach the point of being fully 'renewed'. In our relationships and in the context of our community we are forever changing. But if we carry with us a mindset of renewal, then we can view this ongoing change as something positive. It calls us to continual growth. It invites us to look at the circumstances of our lives and those around us to see where God is calling us to action. It brings us deeper into relationship and communion with one another. A renewal mindset calls us to look to the future with hope and to look forward to change and to where it will bring us, together – guided by the Holy Spirit.

Reflection questions

As a group take some time with the following questions, both individually and collectively.

From what you have read and from your own experience, what is your current understanding of renewal?

How can 'relationship' and 'community' be seen in your parish?

How might you, as a leadership group, enhance these two characteristics of renewal, for the whole parish?

RESOURCE 2.2 THE LIVING PARISH

This resource explores renewal using the model of an early Christian community. By looking back to this community we find a tangible illustration of what it is like to be a community engaged in renewal.

We suggest that, if a group is working through this material together, individual members read this resource by themselves. When the group gathers it might begin by discussing individual reactions to the content of the chapter. Once this sharing has taken place, time might be given for people to respond to the two reflection questions at the end of the section, before exploring them together as a group.

> These remained faithful to the teaching of the apostles, to the brotherhood, to the breaking of bread and to the prayers. And everyone was filled with awe; the apostles worked many signs and miracles. And all who shared the faith owned everything in common; they sold their goods and possessions and distributed the proceeds among themselves according to what each one needed. Each day, with one heart, they regularly went to the Temple but met in their houses for the breaking of bread; they shared their food gladly and generously; they praised God and were looked up to by everyone. Day by day the Lord added to their community those destined to be saved. *(Acts 2:42-47)*

> The parish is not principally a structure, a territory or a building, but rather 'the family of God, a fellowship afire with a unifying Spirit', 'a familial and welcoming home', 'the community of the faithful'. *(Christifidelis Laici, par 26)*

The Living Parish

In this resource we are introducing the term 'Living Parish'. As we use it, 'the living parish' seeks to capture a sense of a parish that is more than a geographical or ecclesiastical boundary. It is about a parish that is alive and charged with the Holy Spirit – a parish community that is experienced as dynamic and hope-filled.

We began this resource with two quotations separated by a span of some 2000 years. Yet there is a consistency in the image they communicate that warrants our attention. They remind us that at the heart of what we may loosely define as the Christian community, or parish, is quite simply people – people living in relationship with one another, bound by a common belief.

The Fundamental Questions

In a growing number of parishes today there are people asking the fundamental questions: What is it to be part of a parish? What should we be about? Who are we? What marks us as different from any other group of people in a local community? The quotation from *Christifidelis Laici* has a contribution to make in answering these questions. Clearly the earlier description of the early Christian community from Acts has a significant contribution to make also.

We are what we do?

To say 'we are what we do' provides us with a key insight, namely that what we choose to do in a parish, and the way we go about those choices, reveals something about our identity. In choosing our priorities and where to put our energy, we are revealing something of our value and belief system. By looking at the lived experience of the parish we find out the real values of that community. Using the image offered by the Bishops of England and Wales in their document on collaborative ministry, we would do well to ask ourselves in our own parishes, what is the sign we give to the world?

The sign we give

It might be helpful to begin by returning to the early Christian community, and to explore, what sign did they gave? What might we name as the values and guiding principles of their life together? What do these same values reveal as the community's own self-understanding? What can we learn from them for our parishes today?

Prayer: In the description given to us in Acts we find prayer as central to the life of the community. This prayer, communal and private, sustained and grounded the community in its life together. It is in the context of a spirit of prayer and fellowship that this community made sense. It is this that animated the community – breathing life into people and bringing them together. Their prayer made their identity different from those around them, giving them a context and meaning apart from another community's identity.

It has been our experience in working with parishes engaged in renewal that there is a qualitative difference, both in what they do and how they are as a parish, when they pay attention to prayer. Having observed this in parishes time and time again, we can say without reservation that prayer is both central and essential to the life of a parish leadership group, just as it is to the life of the Christian community.

Sharing Gifts: In the early Christian community the gifts of all were valued. Motivated by a mutual respect and love, here was a community where each member shared what he/she had to contribute, presumably not just in material possessions, and where each member had his/her own needs met within the context of the community. The other side of this equation is that the needs within the community were named and met. There was a conscious outreach to those in need. There is a conveyed sense of mutual equality and dignity behind this care for all the members of the community. Presumably prior to strategies or mechanisms for naming needs, there was a common respect for every member, both in the wants and giftedness of their lives.

It is helpful to remember that, in order to share what we have, there are a number of steps that must be followed. I must at some stage 1) recognise what it is I have to share, 2) acknowledge that it is worth sharing, and 3) find an appropriate means of sharing. To translate this into a parish context if, as in the early church, we are admitting that every single member has something to contribute we need to ask, how are we naming, affirming and sharing these gifts within the parish?

In the parish of today the respect that allows us to name our needs and share out gifts is rooted in our baptism, a baptism that makes us all radically equal – in the spirit of Galatians where there is neither slave nor free, male or female. 'For all of us are the children of God, through faith in Christ Jesus' (Gal 3:26) – yesterday and today.

Of one heart: We know that Luke was describing a real community so it was bound to have experienced the normal struggles and conflicts found in any group. Yet at the centre of their life was a unity of heart, a common starting point and grounding that drew them together. Their identity as a community was more than a notional reality – it was a heart reality, striking at the very core of who they were as a people. It transformed them into a community 'afire with a unifying Spirit'. This unity is what Jesus hoped for God's people: 'That they may become perfectly one, so that the world may know that you have sent me, and have loved them as you love me.' (Jn 17:23)

In parishes today we need to sit with one another with enough patience and enough love to discover this one heart. It means that when we are confronted with the normal challenges of community, the disagreements, the differing opinions, the clashes of personality, we are called not to despair but to trust – to trust that there is a common ground shared by all if we are willing to discover it together. This one heart is a heart inspired and enlivened by the one Spirit.

Attractive: The way of life as experienced by this community held enough attraction to draw others to it. It was not a community of hardship and despair but rather a community of life and hope. It was a source of light for those who looked on. It engaged people and invited them to enter into its pattern of being. To those who looked on, it was 'a familial and welcoming home'.

There is a fundamental stance taken in this vision in regard to evangelisation. This topic will be dealt with later in this book, but for now it is important to note that evangelisation begins with ourselves, with who we are. It does not place demands on the individual on the 'outside', but rather it offers a challenge and an invitation to those on the 'inside' to become who they are called to be. In today's parish evangelisation is about the witness we give, the source of light and hope we are to people around us. We would do well to ask ourselves what exactly we would hope this witness to be. In the life of the parish, where and how are we revealing ourselves to be a source of light, hope and attractiveness?

This appeal to our 'attractiveness' cannot deny the other side of our being community together. Any community, if it is to live in honesty, will have to embrace this other, perhaps less pleasant side of who it is – not so that it may continue to be so, but so that the community can overcome it. Just as the early community had to be confronted with its own prejudices and sins (1 Cor 1:10ff; 1 Cor 5:1-2; 1 Cor 11:17ff) so today the Christian community must acknowledge its own capacity to hurt and wound. By doing so, it strives to be accountable for those actions of sin but also to over come them and be reconciled.

Community: This group of early Christians was self-consciously a particular type of community. Each member made a fundamental option to belong and each member found a home in this community. The meeting of these primary human needs of belonging and acceptance committed members to the group, allowing members to claim and appropriate the values of the community.

Again it is helpful to recognise the two-fold dynamic at work in this process of belonging. On the one hand, within the context of this community, the individual members found a place of acceptance, a place where who they were and the giftedness they possessed was honoured. On the other hand, within the context of this community the individual members found that with belonging came responsibility. This was lived out in the commitment of the individual to the community. Being committed to the community meant accepting the consequences and demands that membership of the community brought. Being committed to the community meant choosing to live, to act and to relate to others in a particular way.

Faith: Uniting and underpinning all of the above is faith. This faith is in a God who called this community into being with a new and radical code of behaviour. It is a faith inaugurated by Jesus and sustained by the continued presence of Christ in the midst of the faithful through the gift of the Holy Spirit. It is this unifying faith that marks the community as a 'community of the faithful'. It is this same faith that today gives us the courage to enter into the living story of our community. It is a story that contains much that is unknown, that demands our trust so that we can walk together into the future. It is a story which at the end of the day proclaims that faith comes before understanding.

Our primary model

The life of the Christian community has the search for and expression of God at its heart. In turn, the Christian community exists for the sake of mission. Quite simply, our mission is to further the reign of God – to be a sign of the kingdom of God to the world. And our God is understood in terms of faith – a faith we mark ourselves with in the sign of the cross. It is this sign that casts a life-giving shadow over the span of our lives:

> At the beginning and end of this Mass;
> at the beginning and end of our lives;
> at the beginning and ending of all we do
> stands the sign of the cross, saying:
> this place, this space of time, this life,
> this child, these people, this corpse,
> belongs to the Lord and will not be snatched from him
> who bears indelibly in his body
> the marks of that same cross. *(Mark Searle)*

What is it that we do in our signing of ourselves with the cross but proclaim the one necessary faith – faith in the name of the Father, and of the Son and of the Holy Spirit. All our days are marked with this sign, the sign of our search for God and of God's finding us. It is the sign of a love shared and fully expressed in the relationship of Father, Son and Holy Spirit in the Godhead.

It is this relationship of Father, Son and Holy Spirit that gives to the faithful a paradigm for community. Our understanding of the Trinity has much to inform us of as we seek to explore what it means to be a Christian community in today's world.

It is enlightening to reflect on the fact that in our searching for God we use the language of relationship. Our God is approached and understood in terms of relationship, as a community of three persons – Father, Son and Holy Spirit – sharing one nature. This understanding begins to unfold from the first moments of Jesus' public ministry when upon his baptism in the Jordan we hear the proclamation: '… the Spirit, like a dove, descending on him. And a voice came from heaven, "You are my Son, the Beloved".' (Mk 1:10-11) Jesus' self-understanding underscores the equality in this

RESOURCE 3.1 CURRENT THINKING ON PARISH LEADERSHIP GROUPS

The following reflection is meant to be an introduction to some of the current thinking and practice on parish leadership groups. It addresses key concepts of participation, task and *foci* for leadership. It aims to develop your thinking and understanding of your own role in your parish. We suggest that you take some time before a meeting to read through the whole section and then address the reflection questions together during a meeting.

Our understanding of parish is rooted in our understanding of church. One of the greatest emphases of the Second Vatican Council was a shift of consciousness as to who is the church. Over the centuries the focus of holiness and Christian living has been on the ordained and religious. Since the council there has been a real shift towards a self-understanding of the holiness of all and of the role, spirituality and place of the lay people in the church.

In turn, our understanding of parish has changed. Parish was formerly a place of well-defined boundaries. It was the centre of religious but also community life. Generations lived or had roots in the same parish. People were born, baptised, married and buried within the parish.

Parish today is a much looser concept. With transport, urban development and a focus on the individual, the natural heart of the community, parish, is no longer as clearly defined. Our experience, however, is that the need to belong, for community and participation, is still there.

The common understanding of 'laity' or the role of the lay person has also changed. The 'new' role and understanding of the laity within parishes is not of people who are to be led by priests or religious but as people who are to work alongside ordained and religious leadership in the parish. Every parishioner has a role in the community's journey towards God and in the adventure of being disciples of Christ. This journey is given expression:

- In prayer and active participation in the liturgical life of the parish.
- Through each person's growing appreciation of their gifts at the service of the community.
- In daily life through faith, which is ever deepening and ever challenged towards mission and practical expression through action.

The rise of interest in parish life, parish renewal and initiatives focused on parish development, has flourished in many dioceses and parishes in this country. There are many different emphases depending on local situations but the following three foundational elements form the main part of this renewal:

1. Priests and people work together to create a renewal experience of belonging and of participation in the parish. (For example, through setting up and working with liturgy groups, communication groups producing a newsletter, hospitality groups for new families in the parish and baptism teams.)

2. Everybody is encouraged to share responsibility for the future development of the parish community. (For example through surveys, parish assemblies, personal contact or visitation)

3. A number of people are called to 'leadership' ministry along with the ordained to oversee and promote renewal in the parish.

For a parish leadership group a new understanding, about themselves and about renewal, finds expression through:

Prayer: The group recognises and is committed to prayer as part of its life and as its source of inspiration and vision. This is also seen in the group's concern for the public worship of the community.

Dream/Vision: A dream or vision for the parish is discerned, reflected upon and articulated. From the dream comes the plan with specific, manageable, attainable and timed aims and objectives.

Gifts/Talents: An appreciation of the gifts available. These gifts will be in the fulltime parish team and in the parish leadership group. As the parish leadership group come to a deeper appreciation of its own and others' gifts, there will be a focus outwards to look to appreciate and facilitate into service the many, many gifts available in the wider parish.

Communication: A hallmark of any vibrant community is that members are willing and able to have open, honest communication amongst themselves and with others. Communication is a crucial element in parish renewal. The levels of openness and honesty amongst the fulltime parish team and/or a leadership group will often reflect the level of communication with the wider parish.

Formation and Training: A growing understanding of collaborative leadership requires a commitment to formation and training for any pastoral leadership group. As an expression of the vocation of the laity, this is given practical expression through participation with ordained leadership in visioning, planning and implementation in the parish.

Focused outwards: The dynamic of a pastoral leadership group is always focused outwards, towards communication with other groups in the parish, to supporting and fostering a sense of belonging for all parishioners and towards evangelisation.

Concept 1: Participation

The understanding of participation and the role of each of us in the church has developed significantly over the last decades and is central to how we will practice leadership together. The following quotation underscores the current growing recognition that the church needs the participation of 100% of its members.

> Whatever the vocation or ministry, ordained or nonordained, each and every one is an expression of the threefold mission of every baptised Christian. What the church is – a Body of witness, worship and service, participating in the threefold office of Christ who is prophet, priest and king – is what each of us is called to be. We do this according to the gifts, the charisms we have received in baptism. These differ. But whatever we do, we do it in the name of the Lord in the power of the Spirit for the building of the Body of Christ and the transformation of the wider world ... while lay ministry differs from the ministry of the ordained, it too is a participation in the priestly ministry of Christ and so appropriate in its own right. Only with this realisation is true collaboration between ministries, ordained and nonordained, possible.
> (Cardinal R. Mahony, *As I have Done for You*, 2000)

The above gives a picture of the ideal of participation in parish. In this broad sense, the task of renewal is for 100% of the parish. All members are called and all members are gifted. The task of the church is 'our' task.

In a more realistic sense, in the context of the day-to-day life in a parish, these callings and gifts differ significantly. For some the call is to fulltime ordained leadership in ministry and, at the outset of a renewal process, the fulltime parish team, (for the most part, ordained clergy), are of great importance and influence. The fulltime people are the starting point for any shared leadership and renewal in your parish.

It is true that the ministry of the ordained priest makes most sense when seen in the context of the ministry of all the baptised. Yet, in practice, it is those designated 'leaders' in a parish, appointed by the local church, who are the starting point, motivators and encouragers of people taking on board their rights and responsibilities as parishioners. This can be a daunting task. It takes place in a situation of decreasing numbers, of both lay and ordained in church, in very challenging times for the church in our country and in a situation of constant change.

Concept 2: Task

In the broad sense, the task of a parish leadership group is to be involved in the mission of the church, to preach and bring the good news to all people. This broad sense of renewal needs to be narrowed and reflected upon in the context of each individual parish as a part of a diocesan family.

One of the first tasks is to model a vision of parish and a vision of church. The presence of a leadership group in the parish says a great deal about what we believe church and parish to be about today. That is why we place such an emphasis in this book on the development of the group itself as well as on its task. In this sense the task is being such a group in the parish.

One specific task of renewal is to challenge people's thinking about parish and how people view their role *vis-à-vis* parish life. For priests this means letting go of traditional roles of complete responsibility and control. For parishioners it means understanding and taking seriously the vocation of their own baptism and coming to an understanding of the parish as 'ours'. This is an onerous task for a leadership group and requires discernment, time and a clearly articulated vision and plan.

Concept 3: Focusing the parish leadership group

The parish leadership group is made up of priests, fulltime pastoral staff and parishioners who are willing and able to commit time and energy to discerning, reflecting on and discussing the needs of the parish as well as planning to address these needs.

- Facilitating the *on-going formation, evaluation* and *training* for leadership group members (and other existing groups in the parish where appropriate).

REFLECTION QUESTIONS FOR THE FULLTIME PARISH TEAM

These two sets of lists do not intend to be exhaustive; a parish might well have its own additions to make. In the case of the named characteristics, what would you add to the list?

How would you feel about a leadership group carrying out these tasks or activities in the parish? (i.e. encouraged, enlivened, threatened ...)

These are some of the things a group might do. Are there other specific tasks or activities that you think are needed in your particular context?

REFLECTION QUESTIONS FOR THE PARISH LEADERSHIP GROUP

These two sets of lists are not intended to be exhaustive; a parish might well have its own additions to make. In the case of the named characteristics, what would you add to the list?

How would you feel about a leadership group carrying out these tasks or activities in the parish?

These are some of the things a group might do. Are there other specific things that you think are needed in your particular context?

RESOURCE 3.3 WHAT A PARISH LEADERSHIP GROUP IS NOT

Again with this resource spend some time reading and reflecting on the input before discussing the reflection questions together.

There is always a risk in gathering people together. In any group there are behaviours and attitudes that encourage and there are behaviours and attitudes that hinder. People can bring with them their own agendas and prejudices.

When we talk about a parish leadership group we are not talking about a group that is:

- Dictatorial
- A forum for airing personal grievances
- A board of directors
- A talk shop
- A 'holy huddle'
- A ministry group
- A clique

Obviously the above can have negative internal affects on the group and negative external affects on the parish. This is why it is so important to give serious consideration to attracting the appropriate people to the leadership group.

REFLECTION QUESTIONS FOR THE FULLTIME PARISH TEAM

Including and in addition to the above, what would your concerns be about a parish leadership group and how it might operate?

How can you as a fulltime parish team prevent your concerns from becoming live issues?

What influence might awareness of the above have on the possible make-up of the membership of the leadership group?

In light of 3.1, 3.2 and 3.3 above, what characteristics/skills/personality types do you think would be good to have on a parish leadership group?

REFLECTION QUESTIONS FOR THE PARISH LEADERSHIP GROUP

In light of 3.1, 3.2 and 3.3 above, what characteristics/skills/personality types do you think would be good to have on a parish leadership group? Can you already see some of these characteristics etc. among the members of your leadership group?

Getting Ready for a Leadership Group

Introduction

In the previous sections of this resourcebook we have addressed the following: the context for renewal in Ireland and in parish life today; what is parish renewal, and what is a parish leadership group?

Hopefully you will be beginning this section with some picture of what we mean when we talk about a parish leadership group and the context within which it will operate. But before jumping into the task of establishing such a group in the parish and setting it on a journey of work, we are suggesting that it is of vital importance that some prior groundwork be undertaken. The reasons for this are underscored in resource 4.1, a foundational resource for what follows in this section.

As stated at the beginning of this book, we envisage that the fulltime parish team will work on these particular resources together. As a leadership group emerges and is being formed, hopefully it, too, will use some of the following resources.

RESOURCE 4.I: AREAS FOR THE FULLTIME PARISH TEAM TO EXPLORE

This resource aims to help those in fulltime leadership to come to an appreciation of areas that need to be explored on their behalf – before establishing a parish leadership group. It is in the light of these areas, and the questions that come with them, that the remaining resources in this section will make sense.

Even where a parish leadership group is already in existence, we believe that those in fulltime leadership in the parish need to give time to the following explorations.

We encourage those in fulltime leadership to read this resource and discuss it with either the other members of the fulltime parish team or with a trusted and appropriate outsider.

The first stages of exploration

In practice, our experience has been that the first thinking about shared parish leadership usually takes place in the context of the fulltime parish team. This reality needs to be named – along with the importance of this initial stage of thinking.

If the members of a fulltime parish team (sometimes comprising both priests and sisters) are willing to take the time, they can lay a very solid foundation for a future parish leadership group through the thought and consideration they give to such a group as a team themselves.

In the case where there is no fulltime parish team, the priest (typically) responsible for fulltime leadership of the parish will find it invaluable to take time in the early days to give serious thought to the notion of a parish leadership group. Priests in this position might seek out other priests and fulltime workers in other parishes to talk through the possibilities, concerns and hopes they have for such a group.

In light of the above, we are suggesting that there are some questions that a fulltime parish team will need to consider by themselves. There are the obvious questions associated with going about forming a parish leadership group: for example, who will we involve? How will we involve them? Yet even prior to these questions, we suggest, there are a number of areas that require exploration.

The Core Questions

Central to the consideration is the core question: what are we involving people for or, in other words, into what are we inviting people?

The importance of this question cannot be underestimated. Too many groups have had the negative experience of being called into existence without those issuing the invitation having any precise idea of what they might be about. Such groups are vulnerable from the very beginning. Without a clear sense of what is their purpose, role or function they can dwindle away after a matter of months – carrying with them frustrating memories and reluctance for future involvement.

We are not advocating that there be a strict and limiting definition for the parish leadership group before it even starts. But there does need to be some sense of what the group will be and how it will be on the part of the fulltime parish team. As the leadership group forms, members themselves, together with the parish team, will bring further clarity to the group's identity in the parish.

There are two further fundamental questions to be asked by those in full-time parish leadership:
1) What are our expectations of a parish leadership group?
2) What commitment or support can we give to a parish leadership group?

These need to be honestly and clearly named by the fulltime parish team before engaging in the process of renewal with a parish leadership group. Naming both the expectations of, and the support available to, a potential leadership group within the parish can avoid a great deal of confusion, frustration and hurt in the future for all involved.

Recommendations

What we are saying from the outset is simply that, if there is a fulltime team in the parish, our considered opinion and strong recommendation is that they articulate for themselves:
> their vision of how this group will operate in the parish,
> their expectations of what the leadership group will do and the boundaries within which it will function
> the support they are willing to give to a parish leadership group before inviting people to come on board.

In the case where a priest is working in fulltime leadership by himself, the above questions still require exploration. We encourage priests in this position to seek out people with whom they can discuss these issues.

A number of resources in this particular section of the book are primarily intended for the fulltime parish team. Some of them, it will be seen, can be repeated with an emerging parish leadership group in the course of their formation. The parish leadership group can revisit these resources at a future time in its existence.

RESOURCE 4.2: TAKING STOCK OF THE PARISH

As we have said, prior to thinking in terms of a parish leadership group it is helpful for the fulltime parish team to take stock of the parish as it is. This involves the team taking some time to look at the reality of the parish and what is happening in the life of the parish. After all, the real life of the parish is the context for everything that might happen in light of having a leadership group.

The fulltime parish team might undertake the following simple exercise, the purpose of which is akin to taking a parish audit. This type of audit, however, does not focus on statistics and figures but rather on the spirit of what is happening in the parish and what this reveals about the nature and identity of your particular parish. While aimed at helping the fulltime parish team to do such an audit, obviously this is an exercise that can be done by a leadership group in the initial stages of its formation also.

Exercise:

Ideally the fulltime parish team will set aside some undisturbed time to do this exercise together. Preferably this time will be spent away from the parish in a place of peace and quiet. (A friend of ours is of the firm opinion that three hours working in a setting away from the parish is worth two days of trying to work in it!) If this time is spent in the parish, members of the team might agree to switch off mobile phones and to put on the answering machine!

By reading through the exercise ahead of time, the leading of it and the tasks within it can be delegated within the team as it sees fit.

1. Prayer: to focus the team, play some soft music for a few minutes. During this time members are invited to relax, to let go of any preoccupations they might have at the moment and to focus on this time together. One of the team should be delegated to lead the group in some appropriate prayer to begin this time together.

2. Allow some time for quiet before entering into the following scenario: An unexpected visitor arrives on your doorstep one Monday morning in October. This visitor is a stranger to the parish – in fact the visitor is confused by the term 'parish' and is eager to find out what it means. You

decide that the best way to find out is to accompany you for a week. Because of the short notice, you cannot make any adjustments to your schedule or organise any special meetings to introduce the visitor to different parish groups – s/he will have to discover 'parish' on the run, with you!

- What does the visitor experience over the week?
- Who do they meet in their week?
- What do they see?
- How do you suspect they go away feeling about the experience of being part of parish life?
- How do you think they will describe the parish when they return home?
- What do you think are the primary characteristics they might use to describe your parish?

Each team member answers the above questions for themselves. After sufficient time has been given to individuals, the team comes together to share their answers and draw up a unified picture.

3. When this final picture is drawn together, do a final check-in as a team: How accurate and honest is this picture? This is the context from which a parish leadership group could emerge.

4. Make sure to keep a record of this picture or parish profile.

5. Find future opportunities to share this parish profile with parishioners.
- As a team, when do you think such opportunities might arise?
- With whom do you think it would be good to share this profile?
- How might you go about sharing this profile with others in the parish?
- How might you encourage parishioners to give their own input into this profile?

RESOURCE 4.3: LOOKING TO THE FUTURE – DREAMING DREAMS

This exercise is a simple follow-on from the previous exercise and again is done within the fulltime parish team. The purpose is to help the team focus on the lived reality of the parish while giving them an opportunity to air their hopes for the future. What emerges can serve as the beginning of reflection for the future direction of the parish, but it is helpful not to consider it as the end of that reflection.

Dreaming dreams …

When groups begin to look to the future, very often what they are engaging in is a process of articulating their own vision. Yet the term 'vision' for some can be off-putting and confusing. One friend of ours, a parish priest who has worked for many years to support collaborative ministry in the parishes where he works, suggests that it is more helpful to talk about our 'dream' for our parish. This idea of our dream for the parish captures two very essential features.

Firstly, it frees our creativity. We need to be able to think freely and creatively about our hopes for the future of our parish communities. Times of great challenge, as we live in today, have always also been times of great creativity. We can get bogged down in worries and concerns about the present situation, or we can let our hearts and minds run free, leaving the bigger picture, where it rightly belongs, with the Holy Spirit.

Secondly, dreaming allows us to plan and move forward from our new dream and not from our past. Our sense of renewal in our own parish will be based on our dream. We act out of who we believe we are, along with who we believe we are meant to become. Therefore, as you are getting started with a parish leadership group, it is an important first step to spend time discerning your dream for the parish and your dream for the group.

Exercise

This exercise builds on this sense of visioning, or dreaming dreams. In light of the parish profile determined in resource 4.2, reflect on the following questions as a group:

1. What are the signs of hope in our parish at this time?
2. What are the difficulties/concerns/struggles in the parish?

3. What would you like to see happening in the parish? (What is your dream for the parish?)

4. What first steps can we take towards achieving this?

Again we encourage the team to share on the above and to record their findings, working towards putting together a common dream before moving to question 4.

RESOURCE 4.4
A PERSONAL REFLECTION FOR FULLTIME PARISH TEAM MEMBERS

Typically, a parish leadership group will include members who are also part of the fulltime parish team. In establishing shared leadership in a parish setting, the fulltime parish team can give a lot of thought and consideration to the how, what, who and when of the task at hand. But it is vital, before all these considerations, that they look to themselves and review their own attitudes and starting points.

By having a degree of self-awareness we are more apt to realise why we feel the way we do at a particular time. While this may not change how we feel, it may change for the better how we cope in the positive or negative situations in which we find ourselves. It will also help us to make better choices around what we do or don't do and around how we interact with others. It also helps us to take responsibility for ourselves by knowing what 'pushes our buttons'!

We offer the following questions for reflection by individual members of the parish fulltime team. Members might find it helpful to keep a written record of their responses to the questions.

A fulltime parish team may find it enriching to share their reflections with one another – but this is a choice for each team to make.

Reflection questions

    In your ministry what gives you energy?
    What de-energises you?
    What aspects of your ministry do you really enjoy?
    What aspects do you find frustrating?
    What are the givens in your role as priest/ parish sister/other?
    What are you doing that only you can do?
    What are you doing that other people in the parish could do?
    What do you feel is central to your role in the parish?

RESOURCE 4.5: INDICATORS FOR COLLABORATION

This topic is given fuller treatment in later sections. It is important, however, to address this issue early on in your exploration of a parish leadership group.

At the heart of our vision of a parish leadership group is a spirituality of collaboration. It is this spirituality that is the lifeblood of the group. Collaboration has a specific meaning that goes deeper than consultation and lay involvement. True collaboration within the parish sees us all as co-labourers, co-workers for the kingdom. It presupposes recognition of the mutual equality and dignity we possess through baptism. It recognises that, in the spirit of the gospel, all are called and gifted in order to participate in the mission of the church. It finds expression in the attitude we bear to one another and in how we go about being together in the parish.

Ordained ministers, by virtue of ordination, have a particular leadership role in the parish. In the history of the church the understanding about this particular identity has varied. The vision of the church since Vatican II has once again brought us in touch with the vision of the early church. This vision offers many exciting possibilities to all members of our parishes. In the case of the ordained leadership in a parish, it invites them into a particular way of being in the parish. Often we find it phrased in the image of servant-leadership. This image finds its greatest witness in the person of Jesus, who came to serve. As particular leaders in the parish, ordained ministers serve the mission of the gospel and the mission of God's people. As leaders, they derive their model of leadership from Jesus.

Writing in *People Management* 19 August 1999, John Potter identifies key aspects of effective leaders. These aspects are: effective communication; releasing the potential of everyone involved; setting a good personal example; self-pacing. These aspects suggest that good leadership needs to have a clear vision of what it is about, to be able to communicate this vision and invite others into it, and to model the vision in a healthy way in how they go about their ministry.

For this reason, the fulltime parish team need to look to itself and its own potential for collaborative ministry before engaging a parish leadership group in the process.

The traits of collaboration

• Collaboration, in a parish leadership group setting, demands:

the ability and willingness to really listen to one another,
trust in the wisdom of the whole group,
the discernment and release of the gifts of one another,
looking beyond my own needs and wants to see the wider needs and wants of the group and parish,
honesty and safety within the group that allows differences of opinion to emerge,
an openness that enables us to be guided by prayer,
a commitment to respecting the agreed upon decision-making authority of the group.

• As an individual:

Am I comfortable with the above demands of collaborative leadership?
#Are there any aspects of the above with which I am uncomfortable?
Can I name any instances or forms of collaboration that I have experienced to date in my life – in parish or another setting? What was good about them? What did I find difficult about them?
Do I feel capable of meeting the demands of working in a collaborative way?

• As a fulltime parish team:

Share on the above questions to the extent that you feel comfortable.
Can we name instances of collaboration within this team? How do we feel about how we work together?
How do you individually see your role within the parish?
What involvement of parishioners is there already in the parish?
What benefit has this brought to the parish?
Is this involvement one of delegation, consultation, collaboration?
How would we like to see the future involvement of parishioners?

RESOURCE 4.6:
SUPPORTING THE PROCESS AS A MEMBER OF THE FULLTIME PARISH TEAM

Where a parish leadership group is set up, the fulltime parish team will need to translate its commitment to this group into concrete forms of support. This will place demands on members' time and energy, as well as impacting their own approach to their work in the parish.

Once the fulltime parish team engage in the process of renewal it, as well as the parish, will be undergoing change. Together with parishioners, the team will discover what it is to operate in a different model of church, where its own role may change. From the point of view of the parish leadership group, it is important that the group will not feel that it is merely rubberstamping decisions already made by the fulltime parish team, or that the fulltime parish team is simply using the leadership group for ideas or for doing what they had already thought out for the parish.

Before a parish leadership group gets underway, and throughout its existence, the fulltime parish team need to check in among themselves as to how actively supportive they are being and can be to this parish group.

As full time leaders in the parish, the fulltime parish team can (or fail/refuse to):
- Invite parishioners to share leadership and responsibility in the parish.
- Affirm members of the parish leadership group as they begin to assume a new role in the parish.
- Begin to model the process in their style of parish leadership and by being full members of the parish leadership group.
- Support the parish leadership group in the wider parish context by:
  # Taking opportunities to communicate the role of the group to parishioners.
  # Communicating the importance of, and the group's commitment to, the new vision of parish to parishioners.
  # Giving real support to the group's initiatives.
  # Working towards an integrated role for the group in the life of the parish, not excluding the group from certain areas of parish life.
- Trust the process and support the group in trusting the process involved.

- Be open to ideas and initiatives that might not correspond to the full-time parish team's way of doing things previously.

Questions that the fulltime parish team might ask itself at regular intervals include:

What practical examples or instances of support can I/we remember undertaking?

What practical steps can I/we take now to support the parish leadership group?

What support do I/we need to ask of the leadership group at this time?

RESOURCE 4.7:
NAMING EXPECTATIONS OF AND SUPPORT AVAILABLE TO
A PARISH LEADERSHIP GROUP

The purpose of this exercise is to help the fulltime parish team, and in turn the parish leadership group, to articulate an honest and realistic understanding of the expectations of and commitment to the leadership group.

Groups such as this can flounder and ultimately perish because very different expectations were held of them and were never voiced. If such is the case it is inevitable that frustration and conflict will arise.

Groups have also died because the support and commitment needed for their growth were never named and given. Parish leadership groups do not survive on goodwill alone. They require the support of the fulltime parish team.

There is an added complexity in the case of parish leadership groups, in that some of the members are also part of the fulltime parish team. One of the challenges for all members of the leadership group is to recognise and accept this reality. If this is done then a real movement towards 'working together' rather than 'helping out' can be reached between the fulltime parish team and the parish leadership group, as all members strive to play a full role in the life of the parish leadership group.

At an early stage, then, we would encourage the fulltime parish team to sit down together and explore the following questions, first individually and then as a group:

- Why do I/we want a leadership group in the parish?
- What do I/we hope that this group will do/be?
- What kind of support am I/are we willing to give it?
- What commitment can I/we give to it? (Emotional, structural, physical, financial …)
- How much freedom do I/we think it should have to operate? (i.e. what are the boundaries?)
- What role do I see myself having in the leadership group?
- In light of the above, am I/are we ready to take this step in the parish and to accept its consequences?

Ultimately we would hope that what the fulltime parish team articulates in this sharing would in turn be shared with the parish leadership group during its formation. Such sharing in an honest and realistic manner helps build the cornerstone of trust in the group. The damage that can be done to a parish leadership group by withholding the basic expectations of and support of the fulltime parish team cannot be overstated.

Conversely the sharing of such expectations and support opens up the possibility of hearing from parishioners as to their own expectations and support needs. This sharing can form the basis of a vision of work for the group. To this end the exploration undertaken by the fulltime parish team needs to be open to change – in light of dialogue with the members of the emerging parish leadership group.

RESOURCE 4.8:
AGREEING EXPECTATIONS AND SUPPORT BETWEEN
THE FULLTIME PARISH TEAM AND THE LEADERSHIP GROUP

This resource can be used with a parish leadership group during its period of formation. Groups may feel the need to revisit this exercise further down the road, in the light of their experience of working together.

It is hoped that the fulltime parish team will have already undertaken the exercise in resource 4.7 together before doing this exercise with the leadership group.

The following steps will help a group carry out this exercise:

1. The fulltime parish team explore the reflection questions in the previous resource (4.7).

2. The fulltime team discusses and shares its own thoughts openly and honestly, and develop a team consensus around the questions.

3. During the parish leadership group's formation, the fulltime parish team shares its expectations and the support it can give.

4. All members of the parish leadership group are given the opportunity to name their own expectations and support needs, with the aid of the questions from the previous resource.

5. Realistic and honest expectations and supports are agreed between the parish leadership group and the fulltime parish team.

RESOURCE 4.9:
THE RELATIONSHIP BETWEEN THE PARISH FULLTIME TEAM
AND THE PARISH LEADERSHIP GROUP

The fulltime parish team has, and will continue to have, a distinctive role within the parish, given the fulltime nature of its position. Furthermore, the priests of the parish are the officially designated leaders and this designation brings particular distinctions to their role. It makes sense, given the reality of the day-to-day life of the parish, that this group of leaders will make decisions and choices apart from the parish leadership group. But it is both necessary and helpful that some thought be given to their relationship with the leadership group.

It has been our experience in Parish Development and Renewal that, in practice, parish leadership groups neither by-pass the fulltime parish team nor demands for themselves a full share in decision-making about the parish. Consistently, we find a natural understanding among members of leadership groups that the fulltime nature of the parish team brings with it implications about making and carrying out day-to-day decisions for the parish.

The parish leadership group should not be concerned about maintenance in the parish. Its concerns lie more fruitfully in the long-term visioning for the parish, laying the groundwork for attaining that vision and overseeing the journey of the parish to realising this vision.

Stephen Covey underscores this principle of good leadership in his writing. Translating his notions into a parish context would suggest that an effective parish leadership group should be concerned with those issues in the parish that are 'important' but are 'not urgent'. These are the issues that allow for a proactive response rather than demanding a fire-brigade response. They are issues that call on the group to look to future needs and directions in the parish and to prepare for them.

The distinction between what is urgent and what is important might go towards helping a fulltime parish team determine whether or not a particular issue should be brought to the attention of the parish leadership group.

Some practical illustrations of what we mean might help. For example, the contracting of someone to repair the heating system in the church may be an urgent issue but it need not concern the parish leadership group. As one person has commented, it is not up to the parish leadership group to find a plumber on Christmas Eve!

Yet another example of a scenario that would not necessarily concern the parish leadership group is that of the parish that finds itself in the middle of February with nothing planned for Lent. This should be an urgent concern but it may not fit into the long-term visioning that a leadership group might have chosen to focus on. (Though the group might be consulted on who could look after this task.)

On the other hand, the fact that over five hundred houses will be built in the parish over the next five years is not an urgent issue but it is a very important issue that should be brought to the parish leadership group, as it looks to future directions in the parish.

Questions for the fulltime team

Obviously there are practical questions to be explored among the fulltime parish team. The following questions collectively might go towards some clarity in the practice of working with the leadership group:

- As a team, what do we need to be clear about *vis-à-vis* our relationship with the parish leadership group?
- What kind of information in practice needs to be shared with the parish leadership group?
- What issues, concerns do we need to consult/collaborate with them about?
- What decisions belong to the fulltime parish team and what decisions are shared with the parish leadership group?
- Are there other groups in the parish that we have to consider? i.e. are there decisions or issues that in practice do not need to be shared with the leadership group but should be shared with other groups in the parish, i.e. the liturgy group, finance group …
- Can we name criteria for bringing issues/decisions to the attention of the leadership group?
- When are we going to share these criteria with the leadership group and any other relevant groups in the parish and receive their feedback?

These are 'delicate' questions that deserve and require serious consideration by all involved. Again, in the case of a parish priest working without a parish team, these questions still need exploration. A parish team may find it helpful to work with an outside facilitator for this resource work.

RESOURCE 4.10: INVOLVING (NEW) PEOPLE

In forming a parish leadership group, a parish team has to consider the method it is going to employ to gather people who might ultimately form the group. Any method will have its advantages and disadvantages. In considering the following suggestions, the parish team might also explore its own adaptations to them in the light of the unique circumstances of the particular parish in question.

Once a group is established the issue of new people emerges as a constant factor in the life of the group. Members come and go over a number of years. These suggestions, then, can be helpful not only in the initial gathering of a group but also in the maintaining of a viable number for the effective functioning of the group.

The task of attracting or involving people offers a valuable opportunity to be clear about the purpose of the group. This clarity will benefit not only potential future members of the group but the parish as a whole as parishioners come to understand and relate to this leadership group in their midst.

But before physically going about involving people in a leadership group, very careful consideration should be given to the overall make-up of the leadership group and the qualities/gifts needed within a group such as this one. The leadership group will carry out a particular role in the parish that will require particular gifts/abilities and strengths. As we will underline below, there may be only a small number of people in the parish who will feel called to or capable of carrying out this role. This resource begins then by looking at possible indicators for group members.

a) Indicators for potential group members:

It is helpful if members bring with them some or all of the following skills/attitudes:
1. Be interested in promoting the overall pastoral mission of the church.
2. Be capable of grasping the meaning of church and its mission.
3. Be willing to undertake a course of preparation and ongoing formation.
4. Be willing to devote sufficient time and effort to committee meetings.
5. Be able to work with other people collaboratively.

6. Have an ability to listen to diverse opinions and to be able to express themselves with care.

7. Be comfortable in engaging in a reflective style of working.

8. Have an ability to adapt to new challenges.

9. Have a good sense of humour.

10. Be able to interact with others in a respectful manner.

b) The need for caution

The gifts and strengths of some parishioners are not necessarily suitable for parish leadership groups, e.g. people with their own agenda, dominant personalities, people with a strong preference for 'doing' and people with excessive zeal. Discernment and prayer on the part of all concerned is essential.

Overuse of particular people in parishes is all too common. We need to be adventurous enough to seek out new people whenever we can. People who have proved excellent serving in a particular ministry in the parish cannot be automatically assumed suitable for a leadership group – it might also be a disservice to both them and the people they serve by diverting their energy and gifts from where they have blossomed.

The work of a leadership group has more of an emphasis on visioning than on doing. This will suit some people and will not suit others. This fact needs to be honestly faced when looking for membership for the group.

c) The wisdom of experience

The experience of parish leadership groups across the country now strongly suggests that not everyone is suited to this group. When working toward a parish leadership group the best advice is to look for the right people rather than to look for the right number of people.

The right people are out there. Those carrying out the recruitment process, however, need to be very clear, both in their own minds and in their communication to parishioners, about the leadership group's function within the parish.

The right people in a single parish might be very few. This fact should not discourage those in fulltime leadership. It is far better to have a small number of the appropriate people than a large number of people who are ultimately not suited to or comfortable in this role.

d) Numbers in a Parish Leadership Group:

While allowing for the above key point, generally a leadership group will have 10-20 members. This allows for the reality that not all will be able to come to every meeting. A good working number for any group tends to lie in the 10-15 number ranges.

e) Different methods of involving new people

Note: There are many ways to recruit members for a group. However, we will say again that there may be a relatively small number of people in the parish who are suited to this particular group. Those responsible for the recruitment of members will need to resist the temptation to get a set number of people and to think in terms of getting the right people.

Below are a variety of methods that parishes have employed in recent years. There are advantages and disadvantages to be found in all of them. Some are more suited than others to the recruitment for a leadership group. The list of advantages and disadvantages after each method is not exhaustive.

Parish Consultation: The parish is consulted through a parish assembly, parish survey or listening exercise. Through these activities the needs of the parish are surfaced while people are given the opportunity to express their views about the parish. Any one of these activities can lead to the formation of interest groups in response to the needs of the parish. In time some of the members of these interest groups could form the nucleus of a parish leadership group.

Advantages: Everyone is invited to participate; it provides opportunities for the parish wider than for the leadership group.

Disadvantages: The organisation and promotion of any one of these consultation methods can be a lot of work.

Parish Course: Parishioners are invited to a course that has a parish leadership component to it, i.e. *Called By Name.* Again such a course may form the basis for gathering a nucleus of people into a leadership group. On the last night of the course, people could be informed of an extra meeting that will take place to discuss the parish leadership group. Any interested people could be welcomed to this meeting; alternatively some of the participants might be personally invited to this extra meeting.

Advantages: People are given an overall introduction to current ideas and a chance to get to know other parishioners, which may encourage them to continue as part of a leadership group.

Disadvantages: People may have all sorts of reasons for coming to such a course. Unless people know exactly why they are on the course there may be very little take up afterwards and it might even appear an unfair expectation upon them; 'interested people' does not automatically translate into 'appropriate people' for a leadership group.

Personal Invitation: In the case of a new group, the fulltime parish team discern the number of people they need, the gifts they are looking for and, in the light of both these considerations, possible parishioners to ask. In turn they go about personally inviting these named parishioners to undergo training for a parish leadership group. At the end of this training the parishioner can decide whether he/she wishes to continue in the group.

In the case of an existing leadership group looking for new people, the group might discern the needs/gaps in the group and then draw up a list of people to fill the need. Members of the group then ask these people personally.

Advantages: Because either the fulltime parish team or the leadership group knows the people, they are more likely to be suitable.

Disadvantages: This approach can create a clique within the parish or at least the perception of a clique.

Invitation from the pulpit: Someone, either a member of an existing leadership group, a member of the parish fulltime team or an outsider, speaks at Mass about renewal and the leadership group while asking for new members. The speaker suggests that interested people have a chat with him/her after Mass.

Advantages: In the case of an outsider, people see a new face; the invitation is open to all members of the parish.

Disadvantages: Unsuitable people may volunteer; only people who attend church hear the invitation.

Elections: Parishioners are informed about the future/existing leadership group – its role and the task of its members. The gifts needed by members

are illustrated to parishioners. People are then nominated and seconded (perhaps their pictures are displayed at the back of the church). Elections then take place in the parish.
Advantages: New, unknown people can emerge.
Disadvantages: Unsuitable people may be proposed/elected.

Questionnaires: A variation on the election approach is to have questionnaires at Mass asking about parish needs and concerns and asking for nominations of people suitable to be involved.
Advantages: New, unknown people can emerge.
Disadvantages: Unsuitable people may be proposed.

A Homily Time Sign Up: This entails parishioners filling in a card or sheet at the time usually given to the homily. On this sheet, they indicate where they feel they can help in the parish through existing ministries or in a leadership group.
Advantages: People who attend the church offer their gifts to a particular ministry or the leadership group.
Disadvantages: It does not ensure suitable volunteers to the leadership group; it only reaches those who attend the particular Masses involved.

A particular issue: Sometimes a leadership group emerges as a by-product of a parish dealing with a particular issue. In recent years we find a good example of this in parish preparations and celebration of the jubilee year. Other important issues for the local community can bring people together and lead to long-term involvement for some.
Advantages: People like to 'do'; it can be an easy introduction to one aspect of leadership in the parish; the group/parish will have the benefit of the learning from this experience of working together in the future;
Disadvantages: There can be an over-emphasis on 'doing' to the detriment of 'reflection'; in addressing this imbalance, it can lead to frustration for 'doers' in a more leadership oriented group.

Note:

As has been said, the advantages and disadvantages highlighted in each of the above approaches are not exhaustive. One approach might be perceived as being very selective while another approach might be seen as running the risk of attracting people who are not suitable to the particular task of the leadership group. Because of this it is a good idea to explore the advantages and disadvantages to any approach and to make necessary adaptations in light of these, as deemed appropriate.

SECTION FIVE

Coming together as a Parish Leadership Group

Introduction

In entitling this section 'Coming Together' we are presuming that the people exploring this and subsequent sections are already in the process of forming a leadership group within the parish. This group of people will consist of both parishioners and members of the fulltime parish team, who are coming together as a parish leadership group.

As stated in the introduction to this book, we suggest that the fulltime parish team explore the first four sections by themselves. As we begin section five we anticipate that the readership has now widened to include parishioners who are or who will be part of the parish leadership group. And so we begin this section with an invitation to revisit the first four!

We consider much of the material in these first four sections to be of benefit to a parish leadership group in formation – while some of it is quite specific to the fulltime parish team (particularly in section four itself).

A parish leadership group will not emerge without effort. In the parish context, we presume that some thought and consideration will be given to how the parish leadership group's formation and training will take place. To help facilitate this formation, we invite those who are responsible for this group's formation to revisit these initial sections with the following questions in mind:

What resources would be useful to a group at this stage of its formation?
In what order will we use these resources and when?
What resources would be useful to recommend for home reading?
What resources would be useful to do at a later stage? When?
What questions do group members already have?
Are there resources to help answer these questions?
Will we use an outside facilitator for any of these resources?

Planning a programme of formation and training at this stage, in consultation with the group, is of huge importance and will lay the foundation for a solid parish leadership group in the future.

Introduction to Section Five Resources

As you explore this section of the resourcebook, we anticipate that as a leadership group you have already explored together many of the resources in the first four sections. This will have included looking to the notions of parish and renewal in Ireland today, the role of the parish leadership group, and its relationship to the fulltime parish team. As we continue in this book we are now turning to the notion of 'giftedness' within the parish. Giftedness refers to the particular and innate skills and talents, abilities and positive attitudes that each of us possesses.

One of the fundamental principles of our vision, or dream, of parish is that within every parish lie the gifts needed for the full fruition of that parish. Everyone is gifted. Each of us has been gifted with particular skills, attitudes and talents that can be used for the common good. It is up to us as a community to begin to name, affirm and share these gifts for one another. To choose not to is to lessen what we are called to become as a Christian community.

The reality is that in every parish there is a myriad of skills and gifts that go untapped because they have not been recognised. There is a great tendency to downplay our own gifts out of a sense of humility or modesty. But our starting point needs to change. We need to begin from a point of exploring what God-given gifts are available to us as a community rather than what *I* can offer. All our gifts have been given to us – to be shared.

Of course, everyone is not gifted in the same way. Some people will have skills that others do not have. We believe that there are people in every parish who have the gifts and skills needed to be a member of a leadership group; we do not believe, however, that everyone in the parish has them.

A growing need we see in parish leadership groups is the need to release the untapped gifts for leadership within them and within their parishes. It is these gifts that make sense of having a parish leadership group in the first place. We believe that every parish has people within it who have the skills and gifts to take on a leadership role in the parish. But we believe that these gifts will never reach their full potential for the life of the parish until we begin to name them for one another.

It is because of the importance of the above that the resources of section five explore the notion of gifts within the community and the gifts for leadership.

RESOURCE 5.1 WHAT ARE GIFTS?

This resource explores different types of gifts. This will help us to identify the variety of gifts around us. Again this resource concludes with some discussion questions for the group.

In *Building Community*, Loughlan Sofield, Rosine Hammett and Carroll Juliano (Ave Maria Press, Notre Dame, 1998) consider three categories of gifts:

Gifts of faith experience. By these are meant those special moments of grace, times of deep contemplation, moments of insight in prayer and gifts which are the result of one's ongoing relationship with God. Once we have experienced these moments we carry the gift of the experience with us.

Natural gifts. These are gifts that we all have, and that we develop and use differently. We can possibly see them more clearly in others, e.g. the gift of listening, humour, gentleness, learning, being able to fix things, hospitality. We can often be very dismissive or flippant about these gifts in ourselves and it may be good to list and reflect on these as God given and for the service of the community.

Gifts from life's experience. This area of giftedness has to do with our life story. Those life experiences, either formal or informal, give us a unique experience and perspective on life. They can be very joyful experiences, for example, love, parenthood, education, or very painful ones, for example, separation, bereavement, struggle with addiction. These experiences are also gifts from God and are also of tremendous importance to be shared in any living parish.

Questions for reflection and discussion
Can you name any gifts given to you individually in each of the three above categories?
Does the above present a different way of seeing gifts in the parish?
How do you feel about seeing the above categories as 'gifts'?

RESOURCE 5.2 GIFTEDNESS AS THE BASIS OF COLLABORATIVE LEADERSHIP

This resource, together with the introduction to section five, might serve to open up an initial discussion about gifts. It is concluded by some reflection questions to further aid discussion.

Reflection

- Sometimes we can find it hard to consider our own gifts; it is easier to name our faults. With regard to parish leadership, lay people in particular can feel they have little to offer. For a parish leadership group to carry out its role within the parish with confidence, it is essential to start to have some sense of thei gifts of its members.

- We have met many people, men and women who work bringing up their families, managing companies, caring for people in the community but who feel that the job of 'running' the parish is for the priests because they are the only ones who know how to do it.

- It is often the case at a parish assembly or leadership meeting that a particular group is singled out as having particular needs, perhaps people who have suffered bereavement. In concentrating only on their needs, we fail to consider and to recognise the profound experience these people have had and therefore the wealth of giftedness they bring to our parish. The life of your parish, the potential of your parish, is held in the varying and God given gifts, which all parishioners have.

- The reality of a gift is that we have been given it to be shared. We believe that we have all been given many gifts from God, including the gift of baptism. However, before a gift can be shared it has to be accepted. The living parish is a place where gifts can be unwrapped. We all know of people who do not believe that they have anything to offer, who because of background or life experience do not believe they are gifted. The living parish is a place to encourage the unwrapping and full use of these gifts.

- As a parish unwraps these gifts, its members can then begin to work together to use them to their full potential, for the good of the parish and its parishioners.

Reflection questions:
Why do you think that it is hard to name our gifts?
What are some of the consequences of not naming our gifts?

RESOURCE 5.3 A GIFT DISCERNMENT EXERCISE

The following exercise is an opportunity for all in the group to focus on talents, their meaning, diversity and usefulness today.

1. Start by lighting a candle and inviting yourselves into God's presence.

2. Take a few moments to look around the group you are with and make a mental note for yourself of one gift you see in each person. (Alternatively it may be helpful to make written notes of these.)

3. Then someone in the group slowly reads the following text: Mt 25 Parable of the talents.

4. Group members then take about 10-15 minutes to reflect on the word of God with the help of the following questions: (Instrumental music might be softly played in the background during this reflection time)
What is this parable saying to us about the gifts/talents that we have?
What is it saying to our parish today?

5. After some time, invite responses from each member of the group.

6. You might also ask the group to name the gifts from the opening exercise.

7. To draw the exercise to a close, pray together:
Lord,
You have given each of us wonderful gifts and talents.
We thank you for the abundant gifts within this group.
Help us to be good stewards of our gifts and enablers of the gifts of others. Help us to be mindful of the gifts present in our whole parish and to find ways to encourage and support and challenge these. We ask this through Christ Our Lord, Amen.

RESOURCE 5.4 AN EXERCISE IN NAMING GIFTS

The following offers a non-threatening approach to naming gifts within the leadership group. Participants should know ahead of time that they will not be reading out their own gifts.

1. Take some time (15-20 minutes) in silence, perhaps light a candle, and allow people to be comfortable while they meditate on the gifts that God has given to them. It might be helpful to think in terms of:

God has given me ...... which has made me ......for other people.
(e.g. God has given me laughter which has made me bring joy to other people.)

2. Ask each person to record his/her gift(s) on a piece of paper. These papers can be placed on a table or on the floor around the candle.

3. Then ask each person to pick up a piece of paper (not their own) and to read out the gift recorded.

4. End by praying the Our Father

An alternative exercise:

1. Take some time (15-20 minutes) in silence, perhaps light a candle, and ensure that people are comfortable while they meditate on the gifts that God has given to other members of the group. It might be helpful to think in terms of:

God has given N. ...... which has made him/her ...... for other people.
(e.g. God has given N. kindness which has made him/her a caring person for other people.)

2. Ask each person to record one gift for each member on a piece of paper. These papers can be placed on a table or on the floor around the candle.

3. Then ask each person to pick up a piece of paper and to read out the gifts recorded.

4. End by praying the Our Father

RESOURCE 5.5: GIFTS FOR EFFECTIVE GROUPS

This exercise explores some of the gifts and preferences that group members have that will affect how the group works. It begins with some reading material and is followed by a group exercise, based on the material.

Reflection

For a group to work well it needs a variety of people. As we have said earlier, a leadership group will need to be focused on reflecting, planning and discerning as well as action: These different tasks will require different skills so that a group will be best served by its members having a variety of skills.

Ideally a group will be able to say about itself: 'Some of us are good at planning; some of us are good at visioning and seeing where we should be heading; some of us are very good peacekeepers and harmonisers within the group; some of us are good at putting the plans of the group into operation.'

A group that is full of vision people may spend its time examining the wider picture and may know exactly where the parish should be heading but it may never get started on getting there.

Other groups will be very action orientated and will be great at doing one task after another. However, they may resist or be reluctant to sit down and think about how all their 'doing' fits into the overall plan for the parish and whether or not, while they are doing good things, they are doing the right things!

The above is of course a caricature but nonetheless any group needs a variety of people. It can be an interesting, telling and often amusing exercise for the group to explore the variety within their own group. Of course all of us contain elements of all the types but we generally have preference or leaning towards one of the following:

Vision person: this person keeps thinking of new ideas and is good at keeping the 'bigger picture' or the vision of the parish in mind.

Planners. These people are good at setting out the steps to turn the good ideas into plans. They tend to be able to see the direction and steps involved.

Implementers. These people get things done and deal with the practical implementation of the plan into action.

Harmonisers. These people tend to be good listeners who recognise the feelings in the group. They can affirm difference and help the group move forward in decision-making, particularly when a situation is tense.

Group exercise:

1. Identify which person you are in the main.

2. If there are enough people (10 or more) divide into the different groups. In these groups discuss the advantages and disadvantages for a parish leadership group of having each type. (If there is only one person of a particular type they will need to join one of the smaller groups, making sure that he/she has an opportunity to share in the group.)

3. Coming back into the larger group, share the named advantages and disadvantages of having each type.

4. In the large group ask yourselves the following question: What is the balance of each type in our group and what are we going to do about it? (If one type of person, for example a planner, is absent or in short supply, this does not necessarily mean that the group needs to be increased. It might mean that the group needs to commit to being aware of the importance of this gift in its work.)

RESOURCE 5.6 THE GIFTS AND INDICATORS OF GOOD LEADERSHIP

Again this resource begins with necessary reading material in order to put the concluding group exercise into context.

Pastoral councils, Parish forums, Parish Pastoral Core Groups or leadership groups in parishes have as many functions as there are parishes. Whatever you call your group, a dominant feature of parish leadership is an equal emphasis on 'how' and on 'what' we do.

In other words, how we run our meetings, how we make decisions, how we decide the agenda, how we pray together, and how we treat each other, is as important as what we decide to do in and for our parish. This basic principle has implications for us when:
a) We look to the particular gifts needed for a parish leadership group, and
b) When we look at indicators of good leadership that we might find in a leadership group.

The gift of leadership

It is neither possible nor desirable for us to prescribe what gifts are needed for a leadership group. Although there may be roles assigned or designated within a group, the group as a whole is responsible for leadership. There are times in a group when different elements of leadership are needed. From resource 5.5 above we can see that at times there is the need for getting on with tasks where as at other times we need our visionaries to keep us focused on the long view.

There can be no doubt that the fulltime workers in a parish (ordained and increasingly lay) have a particular leadership role. Their primary task, at the beginning of the existence of a parish leadership group, is to be enablers, facilitator of the gifts others bring to the group.

Each member of the parish leadership group cannot be expected to have all the gifts of leadership. What we need, as individual members, is the ability to recognise our own giftedness. Then, in the light of our role within the group, we need to be able to say what we need in terms of gifts/skills that can be acquired through training or supplemented by others.

Leadership is based on giftedness and then training. Being able to say what

I need training in is as important for an individual leader and a leadership group as being able to recognise our gifts and the gifts of others.

Indicators of good leadership

In any leadership group, while never losing sight of the 'how', effectiveness and efficiency are important. Effectiveness and efficiency will look unique for each parish but they will relate to the internal and external working of the group.

As a group, review the indicators of effectiveness and efficiency given below and for each of them discuss the following questions:

Is this indicator present in your group?

If not, should it be?

If so, how will you work towards making it present within the group?

Internal

- Time is spent getting to know each other within the group.
- There is a growing freedom to be one's self and express one's opinion.
- There is a growing ability to pray with others.
- Time is given for both ongoing training and support of fellow leaders.
- A discipline to respect the agreed upon schedule and length of meetings is followed.
- Time is taken to examine the life, values and priorities of the parish in the light of the gospel. In this way the group members are prophetic.
- Collaborative – the group shares decisions together and grows into a spirit of partnership and co-responsibility.
- The group works out of an emerging and evolving vision for itself within the parish.

External

- The group engages in communication with other groups in the parish and with parishioners.
- Active listening is a hallmark of the group's way of working.
- The group seeks to find opportunities to affirm parishioners.
- Fostering belonging in the parish is important to the group.
- There is openness to change.
- The leadership group is known to all parishioners.

- There is a good level of renewed membership within the group.
- The leadership group is responsive to the real needs of the parish.
- The leadership group has the mandate of the parish.
- The leadership group is experienced within the parish as being pastoral, compassionate and caring.

SECTION SIX

Collaboration: The 'how' of a living parish

Introduction

This section explores the notion of collaboration in the context of the wider parish. The starting point is that collaboration is not simply a concern of the parish leadership group. Rather collaboration should permeate all the activities and life of a typical parish. This is because collaboration is ultimately the 'attitude' towards how we work together as members of the Christian community.

In our work as parish teams, parish groups, indeed in our everyday lives, we can become very caught up in getting the job done, in the 'what'. A focus on collaboration as an attitude that finds expression in the 'how' of your group is an indispensable one.

Collaboration, in the root meaning of the word, implies working together, co-labouring. The aspects of co-operation, getting the job done and working together to enhance the growth and development of the Christian community are important aspects of parish life. Parishes are busy places. There seems to be an increasing amount of things to be done and a decreasing number of people to do them.

Collaboration as we describe it includes lay involvement, giving people a sense of belonging and responsibility. This can be done in many different ways. It can be argued that a parish priest delegating certain duties to lay people is involving them. It has been said that a group of parishioners who are consulted by the parish team, while they make the final decision, have experienced lay participation. But these examples, while valid pastoral approaches, are not necessarily collaboration.

The difference between what is described above and the focus we have seen emerge in many parishes is that the above does not necessarily take any account of the quality of relationship between the various people working together. This relationship is, as we see it, at the heart of what true collaboration is about.

Yet in many instances the area of relationship is the one that receives least attention. Typically, when groups review what they have accomplished, they often ask themselves how they could have achieved the end result more efficiently or with better outcomes. But how often do groups ask themselves how was the experience for the individuals involved? Did everyone feel included, did people feel happy about how things were done, did people enjoy the experience?

So in this section we will look at collaboration: how the understanding and practice of collaboration has developed, what inspires it and the different roles within it. As we have already said, we understand collaboration as being for the whole parish, not just a leadership group. In essence the existence of the leadership group is a consequence of the choice within the parish to work collaboratively. This sense of collaboration will form the basis of the leadership group's spirituality and practice.

RESOURCE 6.1 THREE STATEMENTS ABOUT COLLABORATION

The understanding of collaboration has developed in the church over many years. The following three statements focus on different aspects of collaboration and mirror a development in thought and practice within the church. They are followed by discussion questions.

1. Since Vatican II, a new type of collaboration between lay people and the clergy has happily come about in the church. The spirit of readiness in which a great number of lay people have offered themselves for the service of the church must be counted among the best benefits of the council. In this there is a new experience of the fact that we are all the church. (*Final Report of the Extraordinary Synod,* 1985, 2.C.6)

2. We are convinced that the manner and style of relationships in the church are part of the sign we give, and for this reason we must develop patterns of collaborative ministry as a key feature of church life to come. We wish to encourage all those, women and men, who have been trying to implement and explore such new relationships, with all their difficulties and promises. (Bishops' Conference of England and Wales, *Reflections,* 1993)

3. Ministry in this new millennium will be more collaborative and more inclusive in its exercise. The Body is endowed with many gifts. Authentic collaboration is rooted in the conviction that all of the baptised are given a share in Christ's priestly ministry, and that one and all are necessary for the fulfilment of Christ's mission. True collaboration requires an appreciation of the distinction and differentiation of roles and responsibilities in the Body of Christ, together with a clear recognition of the fundamental equality of all the baptised, ordained and non-ordained. For effective collaboration to occur, each one must believe that he or she has something to offer, and has trust in the gifts that others bring to our common task. Above all, we must be willing to admit that we can achieve something together that we cannot achieve alone. (*As I Have done for You,* Cardinal Roger Mahony and the Priests of the Archdiocese of Los Angeles, 2000)

Discussion questions

As a group discuss the following questions:

What does this tell you about collaboration?

As a parish, how can we emphasise and live out these elements in practical ways?

RESOURCE 6.2 WHAT IS A COLLABORATIVE MINDSET?

Collaboration is a difficult concept to define and is a messy business to practice. Collaboration is far more about attitude than action. It is far more about trust than rules. It is far more about relationship, vision and spirituality than 'getting the job done', 'who is in charge?', laws and rubrics.

Collaboration is essentially a spirituality of parish which focuses on the co-responsibility and belonging of all and is acted out in structures, consciously developed, for shared leadership and the integral development of the whole Christian community.

Collaboration, the 'how', is about the relationships within a parish and its groups and a decision to attend to these relationships. It is a decision to be concerned with the 'how' – how we work well together, how we make decisions, how we treat one another.

Collaboration is not easy. In many ways it can be very tempting to concentrate on getting the job done. So why do we as a parish leadership group spend time and energy on collaboration? It is because, as Christians, the how of our lives is a central concern. How we are in the world, how we are in the church is of concern because we, as Christians, as church, image the love, concern, compassion and challenge of God for God's people today. In this sense, collaboration is not an option for us as Christians. Rather it forms an integral part of who we are as church.

Because of the centrality of collaboration to our Christian identity, this resource helps to unpack what we mean when we talk about a collaborative mindset.

The elements of a collaborative mindset

It has been our experience that a key aspect of collaboration is mindset. What we think about what we do is as important as what we actually do. A collaborative mindset is essential for real collaboration to be present.

There are many elements to this new mindset. Here are some of these elements:

1. A collaborative mindset is rooted in our appreciation of *baptism*. Many people, clergy and laity alike, have experienced a re-appreciation of the centrality

of baptism as the foundation of Christian commitment and relatedness and therefore of collaboration. A focus on baptism encourages us to appreciate that all of us, priests and people together, are essential and necessary for the fulfilment of Christ's mission. It is together, and not alone, that we are complete. At the same time this does not take away from the importance and necessary distinction of roles and vocation within collaboration.

2. A collaborative mindset focuses on co-responsibility. This co-responsibility is not just in relation to the tasks that need to be done in the parish. It is not just because of the expediency of having parishioners 'do' things in the light of falling numbers of priests. It is for nothing less than the mission of the church. As we address the needs of the parish in the light of the mission of the church, priests and lay people have distinct roles. What a collaborative mindset requires is simply this: The belief that we can do something/achieve something together that we cannot/should not achieve alone.

3. A collaborative mindset recognises and appreciates the *gifts* of all. It holds the assumption that each of us has something to offer and share.

4. A collaborative mindset focuses on *people,* rather than structures. However, it will employ structures to serve the purpose of people working well together in good relationship.

5. A collaborative mindset is not a methodology or a way of doing things but it does require *skills.* Some of these skills will be innate to us already; others can be acquired. A collaborative mindset will be open to exploring what skills are required on behalf of the whole group.

6. A collaborative mindset values conscious reflection and discerned practice. Collaboration is not something that just happens but is a process of growth throughout one's life. This process is facilitated by conscious reflection and reflective practice.

Group reflection questions

Do you see the connection between these six elements and collaboration?

Can you add any other elements to the above?

How might these elements find expression in practice in parish life?

RESOURCE 6.3 INDICATORS OF COLLABORATION

This resource is an adaptation of resource 4.5. This time around, the resource is presented with the assumption that a parish leadership group rather than the fulltime parish team will use it.

At the heart of our vision of a parish leadership group is a spirituality of collaboration. It is this spirituality that is the lifeblood of the group. Collaboration has a specific meaning that goes deeper than consultation and lay involvement. True collaboration within the parish sees us all as co-labourers, co-workers for the kingdom. It presupposes recognition of the mutual equality and dignity we possess through baptism. It recognises that, in the spirit of the gospel, all are called and gifted in order to participate in the mission of the church. It finds expression in the attitude we bear to one another and in how we go about being together in the parish.

In light of our emphasis on the attitudinal nature of collaboration, the following are what we consider to be the traits of collaboration within a parish leadership group.

The traits of collaboration

Collaboration in a parish leadership group setting demands:
    # the ability and willingness to really listen to one another,
    # trust in the wisdom of the whole group,
    # the discerning and releasing of the gifts of one another,
    # looking beyond my own needs and wants to see the wider needs and wants of the group and parish,
    # an honesty and safety within the group that allows differences of opinion to emerge,
    #an openness that enables us to be guided by prayer,
    # a commitment to respecting the agreed upon decision-making authority of the group.

As a member of the parish leadership group:
    Am I comfortable with the above demands of collaborative leadership?
    Are there any aspects of the above with which I am uncomfortable?
    Can I name any instances or forms of collaboration that I have experienced to date in my life – in work, family, parish or another setting?

What was good about them? What did I find difficult about them?
Do I feel capable of meeting the demands of working in a collaborative way?

As a group:

Go around the group to get a general response to the individual reflection questions.

As a group, do we agree that these are traits that we need to employ if we are to work collaboratively?
Are there any that we would add?
How might we practically employ these traits?
Is there anything that could help us towards acquiring these traits for ourselves as a group?

Collaborative Parish Leadership

Introduction

To deepen our understanding of collaborative parish leadership it is important to focus on the nature of the church itself. This is because our understanding of, vision for and sense of mission surrounding church will necessarily affect our understanding of renewal, collaboration and leadership.

When we speak of the church, we are not talking simply of an organisation but of a community of people in which God's saving grace is made visible and available to all. The central mission of the church is to communicate the good news of this saving grace to the whole world.

From its instigation by the Holy Spirit, the church has always been centred around and constituted by a community of people. This community has in various ways at different times in history taken on the task of spreading the good news. This community, in carrying out its mission, has always been sustained and enlivened by worship and service.

At the same time, the church as community does act as an organisation. As in any organisation, there have been stages of development and change in the church. In our time there has been a renewed focus on the role and responsibility of all members of the church based on baptism. This does not replace a strong tradition or teaching on leadership and authority; rather, it challenges us to understand anew the responsibilities and realities of leadership in terms of shared responsibility.

From the Second Vatican Council there has been a real emphasis on the role and responsibility of all the baptised in the life and mission of the church, particularly as it exists in parish. This has been a primary focus of parish renewal programmes and processes throughout the world.

This emphasis on renewal brings with it many questions: What does renewal mean in the context of our parishes today? What do we mean by shared responsibility? What does this say to ordained leaders? What does it say about parishioners' participation and involvement in their local parish?

Shared responsibility means that each of us, in light of our baptism, has the right and the duty to participate in Christ's mission. Through baptism every Christian enters a unique and abiding relationship with the risen Christ and a unique and abiding relationship with all other Christians. It is our baptism that unites us as one church. Just as baptism unites us, it also missions us. It draws us to God and from that relationship it releases our gifts/talents and unique calling in the world.

Throughout the history of the church there have been many different styles of leadership. As with the world in general, styles of leadership are undergoing huge change. Just as in business and civic life we see emerging styles which are employed to give an increased sense of ownership and participation, so in the church we see a move towards styles which recognise the gifts, ministry and responsibilities of the laity as well as the ordained.

The following resources are designed to facilitate your exploration, as a group, of collaborative parish leadership.

RESOURCE 7.1
GOSPEL FAITH: A GOSPEL MODEL OF COLLABORATIVE LEADERSHIP

One of the most heartening experiences of Parish Development and Renewal in Dublin over the last twelve years has been seeing groups, along with ordained leadership, grow into a sense of leadership and responsibility for their own parish. Collaborative leadership takes its model from the gospel, from the model of Jesus and the early church. There are strong images and stories from the gospels that suggest that collaborative leadership is an appropriate model for Christ's followers. Gospel faith provides the inspiration but also a model of collaborative parish leadership for priests and parishioners alike.

Firstly, in the gospels we find that Jesus is in constant 'relatedness' with people. Indeed the times where he is alone in prayer are noted.(Lk 6:12; Mk 1:12; Lk 4:1) Otherwise he was with people. Collaboration, for us today, is firstly about a willingness to be 'with' people, to work alongside ordained leadership and members of the community, towards a common mission.

Secondly, Jesus empowers by invitation. As recorded in Matthew's gospel (Mt 4:18-20), Jesus does not say 'go and do exactly this or that for the kingdom of God'. Rather he invites, first, that they follow him and that he will make them 'fishers of people'.

Following the call Jesus listens, teaches, discusses and journeys with his disciples. He takes the lead in getting people involved, in explaining his vision.

Thirdly, in being with people, in really listening and responding, Jesus empowered people towards mission (Mt 9:1-6; 10:1-16). Jesus sends the 12 and the 72 out ahead of him, freeing their gifts and personalities for the service of the kingdom.

Fourthly, Jesus finally leaves them and, in the post-resurrection story of the road to Emmaus, we see the dynamic of the resurrected Christ once again being with, talking, listening, teaching and finally being totally and eternally present in the breaking of the bread. (Lk 24:13-35)

Fifthly, Jesus gave direction and showed leadership when the situation called for it. Jesus was teacher, preacher, leader, example giver, and insistent on a course of action when necessary. (Lk 6:20ff; Mt 16:32)

Group reflection questions
    What do each of the above five points have to say to us about collaboration and leadership?
    What impact might the above have on how we work together?

RESOURCE 7.2 WHAT IS COLLABORATIVE LEADERSHIP?

This resource contains reflections on the nature of collaborative leadership and on a vision for sharing parish leadership collaboratively. We suggest that you read the input for both and then consider and discuss the reflection questions which follow.

Reflection 1: What is collaborative leadership?

The following are some concrete statements about what we see as collaborative leadership in a parish setting. They are concluded by some reflection questions that a parish leadership group might use in its reading of this resource:

- Collaborative leadership is a way of relating and working together as priests and people, where the quality of the relationship is as important as the effective completion of tasks.
- Collaborative leadership recognises the gifts and roles of all members of the church. It does not ignore differences but embraces all as equal, special and vital for the life of the Christian communion of the parish.
- Collaborative leadership depends on the ability and willingness of all participants to be open, honest and communicative. It depends on ordained leaders to accept the co-responsibility and gifts of lay people while not diminishing their own responsibility, especially of the parish priest, as the one given a particular role within the church structure. It depends on the laity's willingness to be involved and to accept their role as co-equal and sharing responsibility for the life and future of their parish. It depends on all to be open to formation and ongoing conversion.
- Collaborative leadership is best understood as a partnership model for parish. Working together means that we are acknowledging our place as disciples, all involved in the mission of the church. Partnership means inevitable conflict and difficulty that is faced together within this wider vision of discipleship.
- Collaborative leadership means a willing commitment to mission and outreach. A collaborative leadership group offers a model to the whole church of a way of being church and it offers a model to all disciples of Christ in action.
- Collaborative leadership looks to the future and makes appropriate

preparations so that this future is experienced as a time of growth and prosperity. A collaborative leadership group will not be content to maintain things as they have always been. Rather it will look to future possibilities for the parish and discern the strategies required to move in positive directions.

Reflection 2: A vision of shared parish leadership

We have begun in the preceding sections of this book to try to distinguish what we are about when we plan together for the future of our parish. We have been trying to distinguish this task from other tasks, jobs or ministries in the parish. This attempt is not to suggest that it is better or worse merely that the task of a parish leadership group is different. It is fair to say that over the last decade we have started to become increasingly aware, of and experienced in, sharing responsibilities in the parish in the areas of liturgical celebration, especially in the form of ministers of the word and ministers of the eucharist. As a church, we have tended to focus less on the role of sharing the overall responsibility for the future direction and hopes of the parish. The reasons for this, we believe, are two-fold.

First, thirty years ago parish was something that just happened. The people came to the parish church; community and parish were intrinsically linked and the parish priest with his junior staff administered and maintained and served these people. This has changed.

Second, theory about groups, communities and organisations generally, has changed dramatically over the last decades. Previously the focus was on sameness and tradition. Think of how your local bank, hospital/health centre, school has changed over your lifetime. There has been a real explosion of organisational theory and group management theory which points to the importance of future planning and development.

Nowadays, the health of an organisation is no longer seen in its ability to survive; rather it is seen in its ability to thrive and develop. This again points to the need for planning.

A new vision of parish leadership for today

It has been the repeated experience of Parish Development and Renewal that the success, or not, of parish renewal is dependent on good leadership.

By good we mean that style of leadership that allows participation, discernment, open communication, honest dialogue and which is secure enough to allow loyal criticism and self-evaluation.

The parish priest has a crucial role to play. He is the one who is given charge of the parish and he is the one who sets the tone of renewal and collaborative leadership. In the past, leadership was very much the reserve of the parish priest. He was the one who had the whole picture, knew all that was going on and was the centre of decision-making and therefore power of the parish. Curates, ministry groups and the parish at large had to varying degrees a sense of what was happening but their view was limited to their area of concern.

Collaborative leadership is meant to widen the view of the overall, so that a group rather than any individual has an overall sense and view of the parish. The job of this leadership group is not solely to oversee the work of the various groups within the parish but rather to offer opportunities for support, encouragement and the chance for all to have a sense of vision and mission together. It is the leadership group's job to look to the future of the parish in a spirit of hope and mission.

The care of a parish is a challenging and often onerous task. It is the role and job description of the parish priest to act as leader of the parish. He is given the responsibility and is answerable for his actions. This responsibility is acted out within a context. Crucial to this context is our understanding of power. William Bausch (1997) is particularly helpful in understanding power in parish. He differentiates between authority and leadership, seeing authority as holding a position of power …

> 'which has ways and means to direct, command and enforce. Leadership, on the other hand, influences people's behaviour and allegiance. In the best possible world, authority and leadership merge. In a less than perfect world, the goal is to hope that authority will become or grow into leadership or, failing that, at least will recognise leadership in others and encourage and promote it.'

Group reflection:

What do the statements in reflection 1 tell us about collaboration?

Do they impact the choices we will make about what we will do as a group and how we will do it?

What is our response to the understanding in Reflection 2 of sharing leadership in the parish?

Does it further clarify the role of the parish leadership group? How?

RESOURCE 7.3 THE ART OF LEADERSHIP

This resource looks at the nature of leadership, the difference between management and leadership, and what is involved in the art of leadership. We suggest that you read the input and discuss it in the light of the reflection questions provided.

There have been two very significant changes in our understanding of leadership generally. First, we now distinguish clearly between managers and leaders. Managers are the ones who keep things running, move personnel and resources around and generally administer systems. Leaders, on the other hand, are increasingly seen as people who focus on vision, planning, discerning and enabling the gifts and talents of others, which by definition includes the gifts of those who can manage best. But it also includes those who are innovators, good with people, prayer leaders or whatever other gifts are required in a particular situation.

Second, the true art of effective leadership is not one style but the ability to discern and use a variety of styles as they are suitable for a particular situation, task or group.

More than ever the art of leadership involves:
Being able to 'see' what is going on, or in other words being able to see the wider picture.
Discerning the central task of the group in grappling with a situation, rather than being distracted by other side issues.
Applying the particular style of leading which will best enable the 'right' decision to be made.
Beginning with the designated leader developing and understanding their own leadership style and styles.
Developing the ability to recognise and facilitate the leadership styles of others.

Group reflection
What is your initial response to these tasks of leadership?
How comfortable do you feel about being part of a 'Leadership Group'?
What would make you feel more comfortable in this role?

RESOURCE 7.4

EXPLORING SOME POPULAR MISCONCEPTIONS ABOUT SHARING LEADERSHIP

In our work, we have noticed a commonality of concerns and questions, as well as some misconceptions amongst priests, about what collaborative parish leadership actually means. We believe that many of these misconceptions would find parallels among parishioners. Because of this we believe it helpful to explore these misconceptions at an early stage. By so doing, future confusion and frustration can be avoided while, at the same time, a mutual understanding on the part of group members can be fostered.

We suggest that a group read the following material and share their reactions to it, noting if it reflects any preconceptions individual members may have had about sharing leadership in the parish.

The following are some typical responses:

'As the designated leader I begin sharing leadership by gathering a group of lay people to work with me.'

Collaborative leadership does not begin with the laity. It begins with the current fulltime staff. No matter how difficult, it is essential that the first step involves those who work fulltime in the parish already, be they curates, parish sisters or laity. There can seem to be a lot of pressure to get going and involve parishioners right from the start but it is wiser, we believe, to take some time to involve those already working in the parish and to share vision/dream, hopes and fears and expectations for the future.

There have been parishes where curates or parish sisters have been left out at the beginning and where collaborative ministry, shared leadership and leadership groups are seen as the business only of the parish priest. Conversely it can be very difficult for an interested curate or other member of staff to set up collaborative structures where the parish priest is not involved. It is possible that the parish priest may allow the group to exist or function but it can create real difficulties particularly around decision-making and future planning.

'Collaborative leadership is about letting go and allowing all decisions to be made collaboratively.'

In the sense that collaboration is an awareness of 'how' decisions are made and a concern for shared leadership, this is correct. However it can be disastrous if there is a lack of clarity about the role of the group and very frustrating for the fulltime parish team if there is an expectation that every single decision is to be made by the parish leadership group. Because the fulltime parish team is that – fulltime – the burden of responsibility rests with these people. In this context the important factors are communication and honest dialogue.

If, at the outset, vision/dream, expectation and a real sense of the parish have been shared, and if the group together has decided its role as leaders in the parish, much confusion and hurt can be avoided. Again there is need for honesty. To expect a group of, for the most part, volunteers who meet for a few hours each fortnight or month, to be making all decisions or know all that happens is unrealistic.

'At the meetings I have to sit back and say nothing.'

There is a thin line, especially at the beginning of the collaborative leadership process, between honesty, a willingness to hear everyone, and the designated role of the fulltime parish team. Shared leadership does mean sometimes taking the lead. It means acknowledging your own position, experience and training and therefore your own authority. In this sense authority is the rightful power of the selected and designated leader in the parish.

The question is not the presence of authority, it is the use of this authority. Authority can be an off-putting word today and leaders in parish can sometimes be reluctant to be seen as the one in authority. This can lead to reluctance to get involved with others or an abdication of real leadership responsibility in favour of collaborating.

From the perspective of lay people, we often find that people are initially very lacking in confidence. Despite being members of the parish, sometimes for all their lives and despite having innumerable skills and gifts, many still begin with the assumption that the parish is the business of the priests and that their job is to 'help Father'.

'They keep asking me questions at meetings.'

We hear these comments so many times from priests involved in collaborative leadership groups. It can seem a very delicate balance between being collaborative, having knowledge and giving information. If you are feeling that you are being asked questions all the time, one of the best solutions is to be open and honest about this with the group. But before that it may be important to consider why are you being asked questions.

On the one hand, there may be a lack of information, which you have, that the leadership group needs to make a decision. If this is the case, one solution is to try to foresee from the agenda what information is needed and provide this before the meeting.

On the other hand, it may be that there is a lack of knowledge about a particular topic. If the group is looking at a particular topic then it may be important to look at formation and training needed. In recent times we have found this particularly important in areas which are new to parish life, like welcoming refugees and asylum seekers into a community.

Finally, it may be your experience that the leadership group keep asking you to provide solutions. If this is the case, it may be important to say this to the group and to remind them gently why the group exists. It is important to remember that you are working fulltime in the parish; the leadership group trust you and your opinion is valued.

'We need a collaborative leadership group because there are not enough vocations to the ordained priesthood.'

In terms of the context of parish today, there is no point denying that this may well be an initial motivating force, both for clergy and for laity. And we have all heard stories of parishes that, left without an ordained minister, have rallied, organised and proceeded with leadership in their own parish communities.

We believe that, whatever the initial motivating force or circumstance, shared parish leadership is ultimately based on an understanding of baptism and ordination. This understanding highlights the equality of gifts and the diversity of roles. The motivation for sharing leadership from the ordained to the wider community is based on the specific role of the priest as enabler of the community's gifts and the role of the baptised as gifted for service.

'I was never trained for this.'

There can be no doubt that there has been a real change in work patterns and trends over the last generation. For many people the hallmark of their jobs and careers has become adaptation and change. This is as true for parish staff as it is for anyone.

What is needed is an openness to life-long learning and challenge. What is of vital importance is a support structure that offers training, formation and opportunity for ongoing education. This is most easily provided by a diocese rather than at parish level, and is supported in the Dublin Diocese by an office for the Ongoing Formation of Clergy and by Parish Development and Renewal.

RESOURCE 7.5
TAKING ON BOARD THE DIFFERENT PERSONALITY TYPES IN A GROUP

As a group of individuals, the reality is that every parish leadership group will have within it a variety of personality types. Each of these personality types will have an influence on both the experience of what it is to be part of the group and the decisions that the group makes about its work.

It is a good exercise for a group to explore different personality types and to begin to name their influence within a group. Awareness of this influence will help the group in its future work together.

The following exercise offers a tool for a group to explore personality types in a non-threatening and creative way.

Exercise

By using role play we can often learn much about how a group operates. This exercise invites members of the group to role play one of ten different personality types.

- Who ever is leading this exercise randomly gives each member of the leadership group one of the following character descriptions. Members do not reveal to one another the description they have been given.
- Alternatively, half the group are given roles and the other half observe and comment, after the role play, on what they have seen happening.

1. You are only interested in talking about the young people and you think they are not catered for in the parish.

2. You are most interested in the vision of the group for the parish. You believe that we need to ask why we are doing X, not just what are we going to do.

3. You always disagree with the person sitting opposite you.

4. You are a planner. Your priority is to get a plan down on paper.

5. You are a 'doer'. You can get frustrated at meetings and believe that we need to get on with doing something.

6. You believe that the group getting on well together is very important. You will point out conflict if you see it happening in the group.

7. You are a joker. You believe that a good laugh will cure all. You avoid conflict.

8. You believe that it is important to name the steps necessary in order to achieve the goal. You are anxious that the steps involved in any event or decision be clearly stated.

9. You are unhappy to be at the meeting and have been thinking about leaving.

10. You always agree with what the person to your left says.

Note: If there are more that 10 people some of the roles can be duplicated, again randomly.

Once members have received their descriptions they need to get into the role they have been assigned.

- Choose a topic that the group will look at together, e.g a day of formation for the group, evangelisation, or any other topic.
- In character, the group begins discussing the chosen topic.
- The participants stay in the role for about 15-20 minutes, without revealing their identity.
- When finished, the group shares on the following questions:

    Can the group guess who each person was playing?

    How did you feel in your role?

    What effects (both negative and positive) might the above personality types have on a leadership group?

    How can we handle the negative effectives of these types in our group?

RESOURCE 7.6

A PRAYER EXERCISE ON DIFFERENT FORMS OF LEADERSHIP
WITHIN A PARISH LEADERSHIP GROUP

Whether you are doing this prayer exercise as a group or as an individual, begin your time in prayer by lighting a candle and taking some time in quiet to open your heart to the word of God.

Read from Ephesians 4:1-6:

'I therefore, a prisoner in the Lord, beg you to lead a life worthy of the calling to which you have been called, with all humility and gentleness, with patience, bearing with one another in love, making every effort to maintain the unity of the Spirit in the bond of peace. There is one body and one Spirit, just as you were called to the one hope of your calling, one Lord, one faith, one baptism, one God and Father of all, who is above all and through all and in all.'

Pause for some silent reflection to let these words sink into your heart and mind.

Take some time to read and reflect on the following passage: If in a group setting, individual members might take turns in reading each paragraph aloud:

• In any group there are many styles and forms of leadership. There are people who are good as managers, who can plan and organise and tend to be task orientated.

• In a group there are people who are given authority in the first instance, from outside the group itself. In the case of parish, the priest is given a role of authority on behalf of the diocese and the wider church.

• The parishioners of the parish also assign him a role, and he brings both of these to the group.

• There is the leadership of a chairperson, secretary or other designated roles.

• There is also the leadership of the wisdom in the group. There is often someone in a group who is seen as wise. They may not say very much but when they do, people will take notice. This person can have a great influence on a group.

• There are those who offer the leadership of vision. They hold the group to a reflective process and they tend to be inspired by the larger vision.

• There are those who offer leadership in prayer. These tend to be focused and creative and offer vital resources and settings for the group to pray and discern.

• Each of us will find ourselves making some use of all the above forms of leadership, but we will also have a 'natural' style. This style will be evident whether we are leading prayer or involved in decision making. As individual members of a leadership group, it is important that we know our individual style, that we know ourselves.

Reflection questions:

Some time is given for individual reflection on the following questions:
   # Can I see any of the above forms of leadership within our group?
   # What other forms of leadership do I see within the group?

Shared reflection and prayer: Time is given for any member of the group to share on any of their thoughts or prayers in light of the above reflection material and questions.

Shared closing prayer: The group give thanks for the forms of leadership found within it: Glory be to the Father ...

RESOURCE 7.7 PLANNING AS ESSENTIAL TO COLLABORATION

Read the following and discuss the reflection questions which follow.

An essential of collaborative leadership is an awareness of planning. This planning has two aspects to it. The first is an awareness of and planning in regard to how we are using our time at our meetings. This requires planning our agendas and managing them so that they serve us rather than the other way around. The second is planning in relation to our work and mission in the parish beyond our monthly or other meetings.

Parishes, like any other structures, need organisation and management. There is a service to provide and necessary timing and structure needed to ensure the smooth running of the daily and weekly timetable. But there is so much more to parish than this. Ask any priest or fulltime lay minister how they spend their time and you will soon see that the 'public' or service side of a parish life is a small fraction of the time spent on, say, preparation for a funeral with a family and follow up.

The parish leadership group is meant to be a pastoral planning group. Planning is new in the church. It wasn't needed in the past, because things went on more or less the same from year to year. But today is different. We, in the church, are not used to pastoral planning. We are more used to *maintaining* and *managing,* to keeping things ticking over. But planning is about overhaul and rethinking, it is about looking to the future and identifying ways to move toward it. The role of the leadership group is to oversee the pastoral development of the parish. Some one group in the parish has to have the whole picture and then plan accordingly.

Discuss the following as a group:

From what you have read above and from your own experience, what do you see as the advantages of planning?

From what you have read above and from your own experience, what do you see as the disadvantages of planning?

What type of planning do you need to do as a parish leadership group?

RESOURCE 7.8 THE HALLMARKS OF EFFECTIVE MISSION STATEMENTS

In this section, we have often referred to the task of the leadership group as to look to the future and plan. We believe that the group is in a better position to do this if it has already articulated a mission statement for itself. This will help set boundaries and a realistic framework within which the group can operate.

Before the parish leadership group sits down to articulate a mission statement, however, we suggest that members read and discuss the following material together. It may be helpful to have read both resource 7.7 and 7.8 before beginning to work together.

Without a vision the people perish

Any group that works together will benefit greatly from articulating a vision for itself and its work. Without a vision of the work a group can get lost in a sense of confusion about its purpose or function. It can meander along, undertaking tasks while not really sure why it is doing so. The group may feel that it is doing work that does not belong to it or, alternatively, that it is not taking on tasks that it feels it should. By naming a vision for itself a group can come to some clarity about its role and about what the group is about in the parish. In turn this will make it easier to communicate to the parish as a whole what the group is about.

A vision for a group, if it is to be fruitful, requires an element of action. In other words, it should be leading to some external sign or active articulation of the vision of the group. To this end, a group's vision often finds expression in what has come to be termed a 'Mission Statement'. In brief a mission statement will contain elements of 1) *what* the group hopes to do, 2) *how* it will do this and, importantly, 3) *why* it will do it. It should be possible to continually refer to the group's mission statement in explaining why a group is undertaking a particular project or operating in a particular manner.

To be effective a mission statement needs:

Quality time in its formulation

If a mission statement is to guide the work of a leadership group for a number of years, typically three, then the group would be well advised to set aside a significant amount of time in articulating that mission statement. It cannot be rushed or 'got through' in order to get to the real work.

Stephen Covey, in his *Seven Habits of Highly Effective People,* recalls the legend of the woodcutter who worked tirelessly, using a rusty saw. When it was pointed out to him that he should stop and sharpen the saw, the woodcutter refused, saying that he could not afford to loose the time it would take!

How many groups do we know who seem to work extremely hard and yet do not seem to get the results the work deserves? Very often such groups need to stop and take some time out to sharpen their focus and that, in turn, will help them to make smart choices about their work.

We suggest that a leadership group takes at least a morning or extended meeting, if not a full day, to articulate a mission statement for itself. (See Resource 8.2 for a sample step-by-step guide.)

To be formulated by and agreed upon by all concerned

If a mission statement is to guide the life of the group then the people directly affected by it must sense their input into its formulation. If they do not feel that they had a say in the statement there is little likelihood of their being committed to it.

It makes sense that a person will be interested and committed to a mission statement that he/she has helped articulate. An imported or imposed mission statement runs a high risk of being ignored by the members of a group.

Whatever the final mission statement turns out to be, make sure that the group as a whole are committed to it and to using it.

To be focused

A parish leadership group cannot do everything in a parish, nor should it try. Having a focused mission statement, of just a few lines, allows the parameters of the group's work to be more readily identified. In the future months, when particular issues come before the group, members can refer to their mission statement to see if the issues are appropriate to take on board in light of their statement.

To be precise

The clearer a mission statement is the better. While the group might employ a lot of imagination and creativity in actually coming up with a mission statement, the relationship of the group to the mission statement should be like the well known television commercial: it does exactly what it says! The language of poetics, however nice, can muddy the clarity necessary for an effective mission statement.

To be realistic

We do not prescribe that a group be conservative and unimaginative in dreaming of what they might do and how they might be as a group. However, when deciding on a mission statement the group need to check in with whether or not the mission statement is attainable, and if it is not, whether there is anything that can be done to make it attainable.

A group need to be careful not to set itself up for failure before it even starts by settling on a mission statement that is unrealistic in the present circumstances and will continue to be so in the time scale that the mission statement is serving.

To be gospel based

Because this mission statement is to guide the work of a parish group, who find equal dignity and mission in baptism, it demands the extra requirement of being inspired by gospel values. When formulating a mission statement we hope that the leadership group will work in a spirit of prayer and openness to the guidance of the Spirit.

Equally a parish leadership group's mission statement should enhance the mission of the church and should not run contrary to that mission to God's people.

To serve a fixed time span

A mission statement comes about in the light of a number of considerations.

(See Resource 8.1) Because these considerations change over time a mission statement should serve a fixed term. There was a time when, for example in the world of business, a mission statement typically served for a period of five years. Given the pace of change in today's world, this is now more typically a three-year term.

Due to the reality that the people on a leadership group will likely change over three years, it is important that new members have the opportunity to engage with the existing mission statement, and if the number of new members warrants, to share in creating a new mission statement for the group.

When deciding the length of time that a mission statement covers, an important consideration will be the turnover of members of the leadership group.

To be used!

Many of us will have participated in preparing mission statements that took a lot of time and energy, which looked and sounded lovely on a page – but were never seen again! A mission statement is only as good as its use. If it is put aside with a relieved 'well we've done that' attitude, then at best the group has wasted its time and at worst the same group will have very little time for formulating a mission statement in the future.

A group might not use a mission statement for a number of reasons. These include: 1) It never had the full support/ commitment from the group; 2) It was too flowery in its language and the group was therefore unclear as to what it was asking it to do; 3) It placed too high a demand on the group from the very beginning. 4) It was inappropriate for the original brief/job description given to the group.

For all these reasons it is clear that good preparation is central to effective mission statements.

To be managed

Management involves regular reviewing of the mission statement. By undertaking such a review, the group is putting in place a mechanism to keep the mission statement before the group as a guide and source of inspiration as it works together. Presumably the mission statement has led to the formulation of goals and action steps. If this is the case, then these too need monitoring to ensure that they are achieved.

Sometimes, in the light of experience and circumstances, the priorities for a group need to be changed and adapted. This may lead to changes in the interpretation of a mission statement and adaptations to the goals.

The important point to remember here is that the mission statement serves the purposes of the leadership group – and not the other way around. A good check-in question to ask within the group is: Are we managing it or is it managing us? The former should be the case. A group should not feel like slaves to a mission statement.

Lead to attainable goals, objectives and action steps

Tangible goals should emerge from reflection on and formulation of the mission statement. It is these goals which put flesh on the mission statement and which will be the tangible signs of the group living out of its mission statement.

One objective is how the group will go about attaining its goal. Naming and undertaking action steps attain objectives. (See Resource 8.2 for concrete examples.)

A list of goals and objectives should make sense in the light of the mission statement being worked towards. In other words, there should be a direct and obvious relationship between them.

SECTION 8

Collaboration: Some tools for the task

Introduction

In this section we will offer some practical tools for a leadership group. These resource tools are for the ongoing work of any leadership group, rather than once-off happenings.

In the ongoing work of a leadership group, the need for a mission statement as a basis for concrete planning is essential.

Also in the ongoing life and work of a group, how decisions are made, as well as issues of conflict, need to be addressed.

Finally, communication and evaluation are hallmarks of a healthy group as well as being essential in order for the group to carry out their task effectively.

RESOURCE 8.1 CREATING A PARISH LEADERSHIP MISSION STATEMENT

What follows is an outline of how a group might form a mission statement in the course of a full day together. However, if the group cannot practically give a full day to this task, the time given to each step along the way can be altered to suit the group's particular circumstances. Some groups might spread the following steps over a number of meetings.

There are always advantages to having an outside facilitator for a session such as this one. He/she can keep the group focused on the task in the time allotted and can bring an objective filter to what comes up in the group. Most importantly, a facilitator can allow all members of the group to be free to participate fully in discussion and decision making.

9:30   *Gathering, welcome and check-in:* each member of the group is given an opportunity to say how they are as they begin this session, i.e. tired, energised, enthusiastic …

9:40   *Prayer:* e.g. *All Our Tomorrows* from *Prayer for Parish Groups,* p.120. This prayer session has been prepared by and will be led by a couple of members of the group.

10:00 *Introducing the task:* forming a parish mission statement:
Recapping the elements found in resource 7.8
Summarise the three main considerations in formulating a mission statement:
1. External Needs/Trends – i.e. the reality of people's lives in the parish of … today.
2. Job Brief – i.e. as a parish leadership group our purpose /job is to …
3. Internal reality – i.e. the gifts, resources and values that we as a particular group of people hold.
It is these three considerations that need to be first explored by the group as they seek to articulate a mission statement for themselves.

10:30 *Group work I:*

Consideration One: External Needs/Trends
In groups of approximately three people for 10 minutes and then groups of six people for 15 minutes, discuss the following:
Imagine that you are given a bird's-eye view of the parish and people in the parish. As you survey the life of the parish what do you see? What is the reality of people's life? What is concerning parishioners? What are their struggles? What gives them life and energy?
One member of the group is appointed to report back on the group's behalf. This could be done verbally and/or with the use of a chart.

10:55 *Group Reports:*
Each group reports back its findings, which are recorded by the facilitator and set aside.

11:15 Break (Coffee and time to stretch)

11:45 *Group Work II:*

Consideration Two: Job Brief
The facilitator invites participants to think about their job brief as a parish leadership group for a few minutes.
He/she then invites people back into different small groups to discuss it for 15 minutes.

12:10 *Group Reports:*
Each group reports back. The facilitator then leads a group discussion clarifying the brief – with its expectations and limits – among the group. The conclusions of this conversation are recorded and set aside.

1:00 Lunch Break

2:15 *Group Work III:*

Consideration Three: Internal reality
Depending on the time allocated this group work may be done in a number of ways. If time is pressing (i.e. if you are behind schedule after the morning), then the group could, using the methodology below, discuss the following questions, led by the facilitator for 30 minutes:

• What are the variety of gifts and resources that we bring to the parish as a group?
• What do we see as important in our work?
• What gives us satisfaction/dissatisfaction?

The first part explores the gifts and resources in the group. It could be the case that the group has never named members' gifts. For resources on exploring gifts within the group see section five.

One simple exercise is to prepare a page for each person, headed with his/her name. While participants are seated in a circle, the pages are passed around and everyone is given the opportunity to write/draw something on each page, depicting the particular person's gifts/resources. Background music can be played during this exercise.

The second part of the exercise, i.e. naming what we hold as important in our work and what gives us satisfaction/dissatisfaction, might be shared in pairs for about ten minutes before being shared with the wider group.

Time will obviously be a factor in determining the approach for this particular group work.

3:15   Stretch Break

3:30   *Group Work IV:*

Our Dream for this leadership group and its work ...

In this exercise the facilitator leads the participants in dreaming for the leadership group and the work of the leadership group for the next number of years.

The facilitator might use background music to relax people and make sure that they are comfortably seated. While the music is playing, the facilitator invites participants to close their eyes. The facilitator then briefly recaps on the finding of the morning – reminding participants of what they named as the external reality, their job brief and the internal reality of the group.

In the light of all this, the facilitator invites participants to use their imagination and create their own dream for the group and what it might be about in the coming months and years. As the music softly plays, the facilitator allows enough quiet time for participants to enter into their own thoughts and creativity.

When ready, the facilitator invites people to open their eyes and share within the group the dream they imagined. Again depending on time, this might be done in smaller groups and fed back to the larger group, or done as a whole group.

4:00 *Synthesis*

As the day draws to a close the facilitator should begin to try to bring together what people are saying. By this stage hopefully a consensus is emerging about a common dream and a common energy for the reality of the dream.

The facilitator should work with the group in beginning to put down on paper what will be the group's mission statement.

It can happen that there is strong consensus on what the statement should contain but the group is getting bogged down in the task of writing it up. If this is the case, one solution is to appoint a subgroup which will go away, write up the mission statement and bring it back to the group at the next meeting for any adjustments before the group finally accepts it.

4:45 *Review*

Before people leave an intense session of work such as this one it is helpful to do a brief check-in with the participants. How do they feel about what they have achieved? What did they find positive about the session? What did they find frustrating? Did they learn anything important about working together?

5:00 *Close of Session*

A prayer giving thanks for the day would be an appropriate way to finish. Some groups might choose to have some social activity at the end of a day of hard work like this, e.g. going bowling together or some such activity.

RESOURCE 8.2: FROM MISSION STATEMENT TO PRACTICE

Once a group has decided on a common mission statement it is important that the group moves to turn that statement into a lived reality. Central to this movement is the notion of strategic planning. A group will need to formulate a strategy in order to bring the statement to life in the group's work practice.

The following are what we suggest are the steps in such strategic planning. When the group has a mission statement, it might then use these steps to create concrete goals and objectives for itself. The steps need not be undertaken in one session. For example, the leadership group might try to work on the first three steps at one meeting and then turn its attention to the next three steps at a subsequent meeting.

Working with a sample mission statement

To illustrate these steps we will use a sample mission statement that a parish leadership group might create. A mission statement might read something like the following:

> We, the leadership group of ... parish, inspired by the model of Jesus, for the next three years will work in a collaborative spirit towards making our parish a place of welcome for its members.

We can note a number of things about this sample statement:

It names who the mission statement is for, i.e. the leadership group.
It names the length of time it will be in operation, i.e. three years.
It names what it is seeking to do, i.e. making the parish a place of welcome.
It names why it is seeking to do this, i.e. following the model of Jesus.
It names how it will do this, i.e. collaboratively, which implies a collaborative approach not only within the group but also within the parish.

So we have a mission statement. It is aspirational but also realistic given the mandate of all Christian communities to be places of welcome. Yet we do not have the nuts and bolts of how it will find fruition in the parish. The nuts and bolts are what strategic planning is about.

In summary, the following represents a road map of moving from a mission statement to implementation:

Mission Statement – principles of implementation – goals – objectives – action plan – implementation – progress check-in – mission review.

Step One: Principles for Implementation

Before a group decides on the goals and objectives of strategic planning it might agree on a set of principles that will guide it in working together. The following might serve as sample principles:

Goals and objectives are calendared.

There is a named convenor or overseer for each objective.

There is regular progress check-in within the parish leadership group.

The parish leadership group makes any decisions regarding implementation of goals.

Objectives may be met through the work of subgroups or other ...

In this way, once a group has decided on an objective it will make sure it has a person assigned to keep that task on track, that it is given set dates to be completed by, and that there is time given regularly to check in with how it is going. The convenor is not necessarily the person who will do the work of the objective. Subgroups will be an important part of the strategic plan and, in the light of the collaborative aspiration of the group, will likely include many people outside of the leadership group.

Step Two: Naming goals

In light of the mission statement the group needs to articulate specific goals for itself. What does the group see as the primary goals arising out of the statement? Examples arising out of the sample statement might include:

To establish a welcoming committee in the parish for new members.

To undertake parish visitation.

To develop links between community groups.

To encourage people to share their gifts and resources.

To explore ways of enhancing the experience of Sunday as a time of welcome ...

Step Three: Agreeing and prioritising goals

Obviously the list of goals could go on and on. So the next step is to a) decide on the number of goals you are going to undertake and b) to prioritise the goals.

Because this group has decided that they are going to work collaboratively within the parish, they may want to consult the parish in way as to the direction it should be going in or the priorities it should have.

So to use our sample, having consulted with the parish, a leadership group might decide to focus only on goals 4, 2, and 5 in that order.

Step Four: Naming objectives for each goal

Once you have decided on the goals and their priorities, the group then has to figure out what is the aim of each goal, or in other words the objectives.

For example, in Goal 4: encouraging people to share their gifts and resources, the objectives might include the following:

To educate/catechise people in the parish to understand that we all have gifts and talents to contribute.

To prepare and carry out with parish groups a 'Time and Talent Sunday' when parishioners can sign up to give of their time and talent to different activities and ministries in the parish.

To regularly use the newsletter to highlight how people can help one another in the parish and to thank those who have helped.

Step Five: Agreeing and prioritising objectives

Again this list could go on and on. So depending on the number of objectives decided upon by the group, these too might need to be honed down and prioritised.

Factors to be considered at this stage include the resources of the parish in terms of people, material and finance. An objective needs to be set aside if it will be impossible to resource.

Step Six: Action plan

In our sample we now have among our objectives 'to prepare and carry out with parish groups a 'Time and Talent Sunday' (when parishioners can sign up to give of their time and talent to different activities and ministries in the parish).'

This may be a very good objective to have, but how is to come about? In order for this event to happen, the group need to have an action plan. An action plan is the 'who, what, when, how' of the objective. Each objective needs to be looked at with these elements in mind.

From the point of view of the leadership group, it is at this point that it might decide on an overseer of the objective who can work with a sub-group and come back to the group with ideas about the what, when and how.

What we are really talking about here is some form of management and ownership of the objective. Ultimately someone, or a group of people, need to be responsible in making sure that the tasks within the objective are met.

Step Seven: Implementation

Once an action plan is in place the obvious next step is to put the plan into action, in line with the mission of the group.

Step Eight: Progress check-in

It is helpful for the leadership group to regularly give time at its meetings to check-in on how the strategic plan is progressing. This allows for the group to be consulted on any necessary decisions as well as giving the convenor and subgroup an opportunity to make any adjustments to the plan itself or to the timing of the plan.

Step Nine: Mission review

The parish leadership group should also check in with its mission statement, perhaps after every six months or so, if not sooner. Do members recognise its influence in the choices and decisions they are making at their meetings? Do they recognise it in the implementation of their strategic plan? Is it managing the parish leadership group or the other way around?

RESOURCE 8.3 COLLABORATIVE DECISION MAKING

Making decisions together is a very important part of the work of any leadership group. Why decisions are made, who makes them and what process is used, all need to be addressed by a leadership group, early on in its formation.

As has been mentioned earlier, it is helpful if the fulltime parish team has looked at its own decision-making procedures. This can be shared with the group. This sharing by the fulltime parish team of its own procedures gives one option but is not an imposition on the leadership group.

What decisions the leadership group makes is important. Again, as we have already said, not all decisions can or should be made by the group. A lot of time and energy can be wasted deciding on issues which are ultimately not the group's decision.

Also it is important to be aware that making decisions together is a process in itself and needs formation and time. For present parish leadership, in particular the parish priest, there may be expectations from both parishioners and the diocese that he is fully responsible for all decisions. For many lay people there is need for a real change of mindset with regard to their own ability, indeed responsibility, to make decisions for the future of their parish.

This resource may be helpful in examining how decisions are made at and between meetings.

Collaborative decision making

When a group is working together collaboratively there will naturally be an openness and willingness to make decisions together. Growing together in collaboration takes time and working towards collaborative decision making takes trust, openness and growth for all involved. But, once again, choosing to share decisions is based on our understanding of the responsibility of all for the future of the parish and on the equality of gifts of all in the leadership group.

It is unrealistic to say that all decisions need the same consideration or that all need the same preparation and time.

Therefore it is important to decide what type of decision is being made and decide accordingly. As a general rule of thumb:

- Decisions which affect the overall vision/dream/plan for the parish need careful consideration and decision making by the leadership group.
- Decisions which will affect the future direction of the parish or will alter the structures and policy need parish-wide discussion and a collaborative approach.
- In such situations it is not only the role of the leadership group to make decisions together but it may also be the group's role to ensure that as many voices as possible in the wider parish are also heard.

Check-in for decision making and implementation

When the group has to make a decision the following check list may be helpful to keep in mind:

Whose decision is this?

Are there other groups who need to be considered/consulted?

Do we have sufficient information to make this decision?

Does everyone feel that their opinions have been heard?

Is everyone satisfied with the final decision?

When a group wants to check in on its decision making process, the following questions may be helpful:

Is everyone in the group happy about how decisions are made?

Are we happy that decisions made are implemented?

Do we find ourselves revisiting decisions that some believe have already been decided?

What decisions?

As a leadership group becomes established, it will be developing a mission statement including its aims and objectives over a set period of time. Once this is agreed and checked out, then decisions arising from this plan need to be teased out, discussed and decided on by the group. Consider the following points in the light of your particular situation:

In many parishes, as a leadership group develops, they will be in contact with or setting up ministry groups in the parish to respond to needs. For example, a leadership group may establish a liturgy group, a bereavement group or a youth group. As these groups are being set up, it is important to be aware of and decide how decisions within these groups will be made with regard to the leadership group. Are these groups autonomous? Are these groups answerable to the leadership group? Is it the role of the leadership group to offer support and practical assistance or do you need representatives from these groups as part of the leadership group? Are you, as a leadership group, collaborators with other groups or enablers?

Situations that may arise

Most leadership groups meet monthly. Inevitably there will be decisions to be made and actions to be taken between meetings. These will be made and done by the fulltime parish team. Most of these decisions have nothing directly to do with the leadership group. However, it is worth considering and perhaps discussing as a leadership group, what to do if a decision needs to be made between meetings. This can avoid a lot of frustration and even anger when members of a leadership group can feel that decisions made have been overturned. The following resource may be helpful in examining people's understanding of how decisions are made between meetings.

Situation 1

The leadership group decided to have a well-known speaker to open the parish assembly it is planning. Names for this speaker were put forward and decided. The following Sunday at Mass some of the leadership group hear the announcement and a completely different name is mentioned.

What might have happened in the meantime?

How would you feel if you had been in that situation?

Situation 2

In response to a survey, the leadership group makes liturgy a priority and decides to set up a liturgy group to examine and respond to the liturgical needs of the parish. This liturgy group meets for many months and does further information gathering as well as formation for itself. The group decides that the first step is to reduce the number of Masses on a Sunday cutting the early morning and Sunday evening mass.

Should this decision have be taken by the liturgy group?

How might the issues be addressed if the leadership group feel the decision does not fit in with the overall plan for the parish?

What might have led to this decision being made?

Situation 3

The parish leadership group turn up at the local school for their regular meeting. They discover that they are locked out as the school has been prepared for a parent teacher meeting which will take place the following day. The group blame the chairperson of the group for the mix up.

What might have happened in this situation?

How could this situation have been avoided?

RESOURCE 8.4 COMMUNICATION

The following resource addresses two central issues for a parish leadership group:

How does the leadership group promote itself and its own work/process in the parish?

How does the leadership group communicate with other groups in the parish?

From the outset it is useful for the leadership in the parish to share what is happening with the parish as a whole. Later the leadership group can be encouraged to communicate through the newsletter, a parish directory, by being introduced before/after liturgy (or a commissioning ceremony).

Consider how the following tasks might be approached by you as a group:

- Communicate that a Parish Leadership Group is going to be formed. stating what a Parish Leadership Group is and its role, etc.
- Communicate that a Parish leadership Group is actually being formed, i.e. how it is being formed.
- Communicate that a Parish Leadership Group has been formed, membership and the formation they are receiving, a mission/vision statement – when there is one it should be made known to the parishioners.
- Regular communication on the work of the Parish Leadership Group.

Where and how to communicate information

You might consider using the following as a beginning to a brainstorm exercise for other methods of communication applicable in your parish:

Announcement at Masses.

Presentation at the end of Masses or at Ministry Group meetings.

Newsletter/Bulletins.

Local Newspapers/Local Radio etc.

It is important for the group to consider the advantages and disadvantages of each method for your own particular situation.

The leadership group and other parish groups

As a group is formed and comes to an understanding of its role, inevitably the group will consider the issue of communication with other groups in the parish.

This is because, as the parish leadership group develops it begins to take on the image of itself as not just another committee in the parish, but rather as a helicopter group which keeps the overall vision and plan for the parish alive and therefore is in constant communication and consultation with the whole parish. The parish leadership group communicates principally: to explain its role, to communicate decisions and to open channels of communication to inform and help mould the group's decisions.

To facilitate the meeting with and continued communication between itself and other groups, the following strategies may be helpful:

• An initial meeting of all groups with the leadership group to give information/celebrate/socialise.

• An information-sharing event. Who we are/ what do we do?

• Encourage co-operation. Recognition of the contribution of all groups and the need to collaborate.

• An inclusion of all groups in any major planning so as to facilitate a sense of belonging and to foster collaboration.

• A day/days of reflection for all parish groups to discern and vision together for the future of the parish.

RESOURCE 8.6 PLANNING ONGOING FORMATION AND TRAINING

For any leadership group a concern with ongoing formation and training is essential. In this resourcebook we have tried to address some of the basic starting point for formation and training. However, each group will develop its own style and therefore its own unique needs. The following resource is offered as a tool for discernment of the group's ongoing needs. It is advisable to visit this resource at least once a year and it may be a good idea to include it as part of your evaluation work.

For any group working together there are three areas to be considered:
• Ourselves as a group of people together.
• Our vision.
• Our task.

Formation/training/ planning

Read the following headings and then brainstorm under each category. If there is a large group (10 or more) then break into groups of 3-4. After the brainstorm and feedback consider the reflection questions at the end.

Ourselves as a group of people together
What are our needs under this heading?
(For example, do we need to spend time getting to know each other socially, praying together, understanding how we work well as a group.)

Our vision
What are our needs under this heading?
(For example do we need time to learn about and discuss the vision of Parish Development and Renewal, time for discernment and discussion of our vision, time to revisit our vision/mission statement, some inspirational input on vision?)

Our Task
What are our needs under this heading?
(For example, do we need to make time to plan what needs to be done in the immediate future, do we need time for long-term planning, do we need time to evaluate what we have done so far?)

Reflection questions

Are there any common themes emerging from your brainstorm?

What are the priorities?

What will we address and when?

Do we need the assistance of an outside facilitator?

Who will carry forward this planning?

RESOURCE 8.7 EVALUATION: THREE APPROACHES

Evaluation is an essential and indispensable part of the life and work of any team. It is advisable to have a full evaluation annually but it is equally important to have ongoing evaluation as events happen, goals are completed or as new issues emerge. Evaluation takes place in the light of our stated objectives but also helps us to see more clearly how we are working together as a group. The following resources offer three approaches to evaluation:

1. A check-in suitable for a meeting following a big event or happening.
2. Annual evaluation.
3. A check-in suitable for the end of a monthly meeting.

1.Evaluating an event

These questions are suitable for use as an evaluation of an event such as a parish assembly or visitation programme.

Give people an opportunity to think about and then share on the following questions:

What worked well?

What did not work well?

What should we change if we undertake this again?

What have we learnt from the experience it in terms of working together?

2. Sample annual evaluation form

The form overleaf is suitable for the annual leadership group evaluation. Section one evaluates how the group operates as a team and section two evaluates the effectiveness of the group in the parish.

Each member of the group should be given a copy of the form to fill in. It is a good idea to send these out before the meeting. It is also a good idea to collate the information gathered. (The assistance of a facilitator for this exercise is highly recommended.)

Evaluation Form

Please complete all of the following questions

Section 1: How the leadership group relates and operates as a team

What type of leadership group are we? (e.g. consultative, co-responsible, decision-making)

Given the type of group we are, the functions of the parish leadership group are:

Ideally (prioritise functions 1,2,3)
1.
2.
3.

In reality (list the functions in their actual order of priority)
1.
2.
3.

Describe your present role as part of this leadership group

What do you see as the strengths of the leadership group?

How do you think these strengths could be maximised?

What do you see as the weaknesses of the leadership group?

How do you think these weaknesses could be addressed?

What do you see as your personal contribution to the work of the leadership group?

Do you think your potential is being utilised well? If not, why?

How would you describe the dynamics of how the group functions?

(e.g. organisation and efficiency, sharing of roles, planning, decision-making, control)

Are you happy with the way the group functions? If not, what would you like to see changed?

Are there any training or formation needs that strike you in the light of these questions?

Section 2: Effectiveness of the leadership group in the parish

What is your personal understanding or vision of parish?

What is the understanding or vision as outlined by the group?

Is there unity within the group about initiatives it takes in the parish?

What practical steps that the leadership group has taken over the past year have helped to realise its vision of parish?

What practical steps that the leadership has taken over the past year have failed to realise its vision of parish?

What parish issues does the group find to be the most difficult or conflictual?

Are there any training or formation needs that strike you in the light of these questions?

Are there any points you wish to make about any aspect of the life of the parish leadership group?

3. Evaluation of each meeting

At the end of each monthly meeting it is good practice to check items for the next agenda, choose some to act as prayer leader, chair and secretary. It is also advisable to give some time to the following evaluation questions:

- How do you feel the meeting has gone?
- Are you happy that we have achieved the objectives and covered the agenda sufficiently?
- Have you any recommendations about how we might make our future meetings more effective?

Prayer: the 'why' of a Parish Leadership Group

Introduction

At the heart of parish renewal and shared leadership is prayer. This is one of, if not the, central conviction we hold in light of our experience over the years with parish groups. Furthermore, it is prayer, and what prayer engages us in, that provides us with the 'why' of all that unfolds in a living parish.

In this book we are putting forward the notion that a vibrant, living, parish-community is such because:

- of how it operates – its people share and live out of a unified, all-embracing collaborative spirit (the how),
- of what its members do - they vision for the future, while responding to the needs of the community and utilising the gifts of parishioners,
- of why it chooses to be as it is – the community is motivated and called to be such in light of the gospel and the community's interaction with the gospel in prayer.

In other words, in relation to this present section specifically, we are saying that it is in and through the conscious encounter with God in prayer that we find the reasons and impetus for doing what we do in a parish and for being how we are in a parish.

In light of this we are in a position to say that prayer is at the heart of parish renewal and, in turn, at the heart of what a parish leadership group is about. But it is not enough to simply make this statement. We will need to explore this notion further and to offer some rationale for the conviction we have put forward.

Using this resource material

We have interspersed the following material with reflection questions for the leadership group, in the hope that this will help it explore this section. We suggest that members read the content ahead of coming together to explore the material. The group can then work through the group reflection questions.

RESOURCE 9.1 SETTING THE SCENE

This resource is offered as a non-threatening method of helping participants reflect on their own practice and attitude to prayer within the group.

Imagine the following scenarios:

1. You are a lay member of your parish leadership group. You arrive at your monthly meeting, only to find that the parish priest will not be able to make it to the meeting. With the other members of the leadership group you survey the agenda and look specifically at the opening item – Prayer. The name of the parish priest is beside this agenda item. Within the leadership group, which of the following do you suspect will take place?

    a) The group decide to skip the prayer in the absence of the parish priest and immediately move on to the next item.

    b) The group ask the parish sister to say a quick prayer.

    c) The group recite together a 'Hail Mary' or 'Our Father' and get on with the business of the meeting.

    d) A member volunteers to lead the group in an opening prayer, with some time for quiet and space for shared prayer.

2. It is the start of your monthly meeting. A member of the leadership group draws attention to the fact that the agenda is overloaded and that in the middle (of all the items) is an important item that demands the group's attention and time. She suggests that the group defer some of the items on the agenda and shorten others. The prayer has been allocated 15 minutes in the meeting. What do you suspect will take place in relation to the prayer?

    The 15 minutes allocated to prayer will hold.

    The 15 minutes allocated to it will be shortened to 5 minutes.

    The prayer will be replaced with the recitation of the Our Father.

    The prayer will be omitted for this meeting for the sake of giving the primary agenda item enough time.

Whether members are conscious of it or not, the likely response to the above scenarios depends on the individual's and the group's understanding of prayer and its role in the life of the leadership group.

We would hope that in the first scenario there might even be an 'e)' response – namely that a member of the group other than the parish priest has already prepared prayer, or an 'f)' response – that the parish priest had contacted another member ahead of time in anticipation of his absence, and asked him/her to prepare and lead the prayer at the meeting.

In the second scenario we would hope that the group would automatically assume that the 15 minutes for prayer would hold. But why might we hope for these responses? Resource 9.2 seeks to answer this question.

Group questions

What do you imagine to have been the responses of your group in the above scenarios?

Why?

RESOURCE 9.2
PRAYING TOGETHER: THE HEARTBEAT OF EVERY PARISH GROUP

This resource is given in order to help members of the leadership group to come to an appreciation of the importance of prayer within the group.

Experience has shown that prayer is at the heart of parish renewal and at the heart of all that parish leadership groups are and do together. Putting it simply, the parish leadership group for which prayer is a vital element of its meetings is a group that flourishes in all that it does, through both success and failure. In the light of our experience we can say that there is a qualitative difference in those groups who give significance to prayer.

However, in practical terms, fruitful and effective prayer in the parish leadership group is often hampered by one, or a combination of the following obstacles:

(a) a feeling of incompetence or inadequacy; the group wants to pray together and appreciates the value of prayer, but does not know how to go about it;

(b) misconceptions or conflicting conceptions within the group as to what prayer is. For instance, prayer means saying the rosary, or prayer means deep contemplation with long silences, or prayer means very personal sharing;

(c) an attitude within the group that giving ten or fifteen minutes to prayer out of a meeting lasting one-and-a-half to two hours is equivalent to ten or fifteen minutes of precious meeting time lost. Let us look at these one by one.

(a) From feeling apprehensive to feeling confident

The first obstacle mentioned above was about a group feeling incompetent and inadequate about praying as a group. It is likely that behind these feelings of incompetence or inadequacy lie other issues. Who leads the prayer in the group? Is it the priest, or the parish sister, or a local catechist? Or is it any one of us who is baptised? These questions are important. Often a group will just presume that it is up to the priest or sister in the group. Even to suggest the possibility of other people leading prayer may be a new idea for some. But it is an idea very much worth exploring.

This is so because, in terms of a parish leadership group, the question of who leads the group's prayer reflects an overarching aspiration of the group, namely shared responsibility. If the group is striving to nurture an experience of shared responsibility within the wider parish then, in practice, it makes sense to share responsibility for the leadership of prayer within the group.

The responsibility for leading prayer in the group does not reside with the priests or with the fulltime parish team. Each of us has an ability to pray. Many of us will have the gift of being able to lead prayer – if given both the tools and opportunity.

Many groups rotate the leading of the prayer and have found this to be a very positive experience. Before a group decides to rotate or widen the leading of prayer, it is wise to give some time to discussing why the group might choose to do this and the apprehensions that group members may have.

Apprehensions that members of parish groups have shared with us in the past include the following:
- What do I say? Where do I start?
- I don't know any prayers or have any ideas/ books/resources.
- The idea of preparing prayer is new to me.
- The pressure of having to produce the best prayer yet!
- It's the priest's job.
- What theme will I choose and will it be relevant to the group?
- How long/short should it be? What shape should it take?
- Perhaps only some people have the gift of leading prayer.
- I'm afraid of making a mess of it and making a fool of myself.
- How do I measure what the group can take without putting them off?
- Fear of people in the group and what they might think of me.
- People may be resistant to prayer or think that we are wasting time.
- Prayer is meant to be private.
- What if there is tension/conflict in the group?

Obviously these are very real apprehensions. Experience has shown that it is wise and helpful to discuss them as a group before expanding prayer and its leadership within the group.

Group question

What is your reaction to the above apprehensions?

Are there other apprehensions that you have about leading prayer?

However one does it, it is important to explore these fears and apprehensions. Some of the above apprehensions are about the perceived group attitude to a prayer leader. These can be relieved quite easily if acknowledged and discussed as a group, ahead of time.

As regards the actual content and conducting of the group's prayer, the material in *Prayer for Parish Groups,* both in its introduction and in the actual resources, is designed to help each member of any parish group become competent in preparing and leading a prayer session.

Groups where the prayer leadership is rotated have already begun to identify and affirm the positive aspects of such an approach. Their comments include the following:

- Each person brings his/her own personality and colour to the prayer.
- Prayer is now more accessible.
- Prayer is as important, if not more important, than any other aspect of the meeting.
- It's okay to have a different style of prayer – there is no rigid formula.
- Leading prayer is not about being a priest or sister.
- Prayer is now at the centre of who we are and what we are about, it is not a frill or a necessary thing to go through before getting to the 'meeting'.
- We now feel more confident to ground our work in our prayer and the gospel.
- I feel less embarrassed to talk about God and faith.
- Prayer is about more than saying words; its about trying to bring words and images to life.
- We've grown in our prayer together – it is freer and less fearful.
- I think that we are more patient and listen to one another better because of our experience of prayer and the fact that we all own it, through sharing in its leadership.
- I enjoy preparing the prayer and thinking about it before hand. I also appreciate the work that goes into it when others do it.

Group questions

Do you think that it would be good to rotate the leadership of the group's prayer?

Why?

(b) Prayer means different things

Obstacle (b) was about misconceptions or conflicting perceptions within the parish leadership group as to what prayer is. Prayer is, quite simply, making space to communicate with God. It is about setting aside a time and a place where we can consciously enter into God's presence. It is about creating a space in which we can both listen to and talk to God.

Prayer can take a variety of forms. It can consist of 'saying prayers', such as the rosary. It can consist of becoming quite still and maintaining an un-interrupted silence. It can consist of reflective reading of the Bible. It can involve singing and music. It can involve movement and dance. It can be indoors or outdoors. It can be alone or together, or a mixture of both.

In the context of the parish leadership group, prayer will tend to be more communal than personal, though time is often given for personal prayer. As a group, the members create a space to welcome God into the heartbeat of their work.

Whatever form it takes, the essence of prayer is always the same – making space so as to be in communication with God. This does not mean that God is only there when we are praying. In fact, God is there all the time and most of us are probably 'praying' in an unconscious kind of way a lot of the time.

But when we make a special space for prayer, we become more keenly aware of the God who is there all the time. We realise that God speaks to us through the events of our lives and in the events of the lives of those around us. We meet God in the very 'stuff' of our lives – indeed this 'stuff' is the 'raw material' of our prayer! Prayer does not take us away from life; it brings us deeper into life.

The conversation that is prayer – ourselves and God, listening and speaking – changes us. It changes our hearts and then our lives. Prayer affirms and encourages us in our struggles, while it can also invite us to conversion and a change of heart. Either way, it makes a difference to how we live our lives.

(c) The importance of prayer – our sharing in God's work

Obstacle (c) above was about the feeling that prayer takes up precious time. People involved in parish leadership groups have only so much time to give to meetings, maybe only an hour or two every month. Ten or fifteen minutes of prayer can look like a huge chunk taken out of a busy agenda. And yet, prayer is the one element in the work of a parish leadership group that is indispensable.

There are many other elements that make up the meeting – the initial chat, looking over minutes, debating issues, hearing reports, making decisions, input, small group discussions, planning, the cup of tea. Any one of these might be missing and the loss could be made up. But if there is no prayer, the group has lost sight of what it is about.

Nothing could be further from the truth than thinking that prayer time is lost time. The time given to prayer together is what gives the group its identity and its mission. This is not something that can be achieved with a cursory prayer at the start or the end of a meeting.

The reason for giving quality time to prayer lies in the nature of parish renewal. The leadership group, through its work, is contributing to renewal in the parish. And the work of parish renewal is the Lord's work, or rather our collaboration with God's saving work amongst us. And here we are moving closer to the heart of the matter. Our efforts to share responsibility and collaborate with one another may sometimes obscure the more important fact that in parish renewal God is sharing responsibility with us. God is inviting us to become partners in the divine task of transforming all things in Christ.

The place of prayer in the life of the parish group is not unlike the place of the avowal of love in a relationship. If love is not spoken, if a couple do not frequently avow their love, that love will begin to dissolve. Likewise, in prayer the members of the group avow the love that inspires them. They name who they are. They declare aloud the Christianity that is the core of their humanity.

In and through its prayer the parish leadership group is giving itself a very conscious reminder of the reason for it being together. It is making, also, a very conscious statement about what it chooses to do and how it chooses to go about its work. Without making room for such a conscious encounter with God, the whole mission of the group will dissipate into the realm of uncertainty, with a lack of both vision and motivation.

Of key importance is the reality that engaging in prayer brings with it the possibility of and openness to change and redirection. If we consciously spend time listening to and talking to God in prayer we may well find ourselves exploring and following paths we might not otherwise have chosen.

So, if prayer is lost, everything is lost. The work becomes simply *our* work. As the psalmist declared, 'If the Lord does not build the house, in vain do the builders labour.' Without prayer the group might work efficiently, but the work will cease to be truly 'Christian'. Without prayer the group might get things done but the tasks may not be in any way related to the mission of God's people.

Group reflection questions
What do I feel about the above understanding of prayer?
As a group how important should prayer be to our work?

The fruits of prayer
The significance of prayer in the life of a parish leadership group might perhaps be better understood by looking to its fruits or benefits for those groups who engage in it. Prayer is the gateway into a world where God and humankind strive together to build the kingdom. In prayer, parish leadership group members open themselves to something that is greater than them. They open themselves to a divine-human collaboration that will bear rich fruit for them as a group. Reflecting on groups who in practice have been open to prayer and who have actively placed prayer at their centre, we have begun to identify the following fruits:

\# Prayer unites the group in a single spirit. With their varied life experiences, members of the group each bring their own colour and spirit to the group's prayer. Though all can be in very different places in their lives, feeling different emotions, prayer makes it possible for all to be in the same place for a period of time.

\# Prayer helps the group focus on its vision and purpose. It brings the group back to who it is and what it is about. A lot of activity can have the effect of 'scattering' a person. Prayer helps us to 'collect' ourselves again and to recover a sense of our overall direction.

\# Prayer provides a setting in which members of the group can share both their hopes and anxieties about the work of parish renewal. The sharing of uncertainties and convictions, of struggles and hopes, brings a new depth of relationship within the group.

\# Prayer yields a perspective on the highs and lows of the group's experience. It nurtures a proper appreciation of both success and failure, by placing both in the context of the Lord's slow work amongst us. It teaches the group to be less anxious about 'doing' and achieving and to be more aware of 'being' in a particular way, as a group whose members identify themselves as followers of Christ.

\# Prayer is both comforting and challenging. When members of the group are downhearted, prayer puts them back in touch with what they really want. It regenerates motivation and commitment. On the other hand, when members grow complacent or self-congratulatory, it presents anew the challenge of renewal.

Group questions
Do these fruits make sense?
Are there other fruits of prayer that can be added to the above?

Clearly, the pulse of prayer within these groups nurtures and fosters their sense of partnership with God. Its constant presence as a heartbeat acts as a loving and gentle reminder of what the group is really about in any work undertaken in the name of the church.

To conclude, once again we need to say that it is our conviction that prayer gives us the 'why' of the work of any parish leadership group. The very dynamic of prayer that has at its core God's calling of us and our response, underscores the collaborative spirit in which we are called to engage with one another in the parish. The dialogue that emerges in prayer keeps us in touch with the mission of God's people, in which we are all called to share. The direction in which prayer leads us sets us on the path of God's work –a work greater than ourselves but a work in which we are called to participate in for the building of the kingdom of God in the places in which we dwell.

Group questions

Overall what is our reaction to the content of this section?

What implications does this have for our leadership group and how we go about our meetings?

RESOURCE 9.3 SOME SUGGESTIONS FOR SHARED LEADERSHIP OF PRAYER

This resource offers some basic and straight-forward considerations for any group hoping to establish prayer as an important aspect of its time together.

An important starting point for trying to establish prayer as a central part of the group's time together is the exploration of people's attitudes to prayer in the context of the parish leadership group. Resource 9.2 is a resource for any group discussion on the topic.

Four simple suggestions

Obviously our hope is that the group will want to make prayer an essential component of its meeting time. We also hope that the group will decide to share the leadership of the prayer by rotating it among the group. If this emerges as the case, it may be helpful for individual members to keep in mind the following four suggestions:

a) Prepare well.
b) Move forward gently.
c) Aim for the participation of all.
d) Review the experience.

Prepare well

Prayer need not be a complicated affair. But because it is so important, it should be carefully and lovingly prepared. There are tools to help us in our preparation. Nowadays we can find a huge array of book of prayers on the shelves of bookstores. What these books provide us with are the texts for prayer. In these following resources we hope to help a group move from a text of prayer to an experience of prayer. We are suggesting that to make the best use of prayer texts you need to use these resources.

This section, therefore, presumes the necessity of good preparation, done ahead of time with plenty of opportunity for thought and reflection on the part of those preparing and leading the prayer.

In practical terms, achieving good preparation means making sure that the person preparing the prayer has been given plenty of notice. It also means making sure that he/she has access to the resources in this section of the book to help them in the task.

Again, the task of those preparing and leading prayer is to transform a text for prayer into an experience of prayer. This can only be done through careful preparation.

Move forward gently

Group prayer may be new to many parish leadership group members. It is very important that the prayer time be a positive, non-threatening experience from the beginning. This means starting with very straightforward prayer, where most of the focus is on using the text and not too much focus is on silence or spontaneous shared prayer.

As time goes on, and the group becomes more familiar with the format, the prayer can become more imaginative – with more attention to the sacred space, more time for silence, more sharing of personal reflections and prayers. Also, as time goes on, the time for prayer may expand; it should never be less than ten minutes, but it may sometimes come to take up twice this time or more.

Aim for the participation of all

This means two things. First, the prayer should allow for maximum participation, through sharing out prayers and readings (or sections of readings) and through time for spontaneous prayer. Second, the preparation and leadership of the prayer should be rotated around the group. In the initial stages, members might find it less intimidating if they prepare the prayer in pairs.

A simple yet vital way of helping to maximise participation is to make sure that everyone in the group has a copy of the prayer text. Although it may be troublesome, the usefulness of ensuring that everyone has a copy of the prayer cannot be exaggerated. It means that members have the texts to ponder during times of quiet reflection and for any spoken responses they might have in the prayer. It also enables members to take home the prayer and to use it themselves, privately or with their families.

Review the experience

It is advisable to check in occasionally among yourselves as a group as to how the experience of prayer is for members. By doing such a check-in, any tensions or concerns about the prayer and its leadership can be raised. It also gives members an opportunity to share what they have experienced as the fruits or benefits of prayer in the group.

By engaging in an occasional review of the prayer within the group, the group remain attentive to how it goes about prayer. It is not taken for granted, but can be continually reflected upon and enriched.

RESOURCE 9.4 PREPARING A PRAYER SESSION: A STEP-BY-STEP GUIDE

As has already been stated the task of those preparing and leading prayer is to transform a text for prayer into an experience of prayer. The following steps are offered with this task in mind.

Step One: Note the elements of group prayer

Obviously there is more to prayer than simply the text we use. Before preparing and leading group prayer, it is important to note the variety of elements that it includes. We are suggesting the following as elements of an experience of prayer. They are flexible and need not all be present on each occasion. Their sequence can be adapted.

> The Setting
> The Sacred Space
> The Introduction and Focusing
> Music
> Reading(s) and/or Reflection(s)
> Movement/Gesture
> Quiet Time/ Silence
> Shared Prayer/ Reflections
> Intercessions
> Concluding Prayer

Some of these elements may be very new to group members. When looked at more closely, each of them can be seen to be quite straightforward. (*Note:* The two prayer resources within this section provide practical examples of some of the above elements, i.e. the focusing, intercessions etc.)

The Setting

A key to deepening the experience of prayer is attending to mood and atmosphere, which is created by the setting. If people are merely rattling off a perfunctory prayer, the setting is inconsequential. If they want prayer to be what it can be, setting is all-important. Setting includes the lighting, heating and seating arrangement of the room.

Prayer is often enhanced by dim lighting (while making sure that readers can read their sheets), and is most certainly enhanced by a warm environment. If a room is too hot or too cold people will not want to linger in prayer. Ideally people should be seated in a circle or semi-circle, and the seating should be comfortable but firm. Sitting in rows, or in uncomfortable chairs, will not help the experience of prayer.

The Sacred Space

The sacred space refers to a central, visual focus for the group. It reminds group members of the presence of the Lord among them. It may be as simple as a lighted candle placed in the middle of the floor or table. It may be more elaborate, including, for instance, cloth, flowers, leaves/branches, icon/painting, photographs. What is chosen for the sacred space will depend on the images within the text of prayer, and/or on the time or season of the year.

As a year unfolds, the following visual ideas or themes might suggest themselves:

Early Autumn: first fruits, abundance, harvest, green, darker emerald green.

Late October/November: green, natural browns/rusts, berries, natural rough fabrics, dry leaves, wheat, pumpkins, lanterns, prayers for the dead.

Advent: violet, blue – royal and lighter shades in contrast, silver, barren, deciduous branches, advent wreath, Jesse tree.

Christmas: Light, white, poinsettias, evergreens, richness of fabric, gold, green, red.

January/ Spring: green, snowdrops, new beginnings, fresh start, new life, first hints of new growth, bulbs, buds, daffodils, St. Brigid.

Lent: purple, browns, ashes, barrenness, water jugs, sand, desert, stones

March: St Patrick, green, heritage, water, baptism, holy sites.

Easter: white, bursts of colour, primary colours, flowers (lily, tulips, chrysanthemums) richness in smell and sight, oil, light, renewal, rebirth, water.

May: Mary, Pentecost, blooming flowers, red, dove, spirit, wind, life.

Summer: green, yellows, plants, flowers.

The Introduction and Focusing

The very manner in which the prayer begins is vital. What happens at the beginning sets the tone for what is to follow. The leader, therefore, will need to give some thought to how he/she will begin. He/she may decide to introduce the prayer. This may include mentioning the theme of the prayer and giving the outline of the prayer. The first words spoken by the leader are key and require some thought and care ahead of time.

Focusing refers to the time at the beginning of the prayer where people gather themselves and settle down into a spirit of prayer. This might involve the prayer leader allowing a few moments' quiet for people to focus on the theme. It might be appropriate to play some music and/or to slowly read the focus text on the prayer sheet, if there is one.

The leader might invite people to make the sign of the cross, before or after the focusing time.

Music

Music can enhance the prayer experience, by embellishing the theme or by helping people to enter into a time of reflection. It can be used at a variety of stages within the prayer, depending on what it is being used for. It can be instrumental or sung, it can be classical or contemporary. If using a tape recorder or CD player, it will have to be set ahead of time and the leader will need to know when to start and stop it. Some groups may have a repertoire of hymns/songs that they can sing themselves.

Reading(s) and/or Reflection(s)

Readings and reflections can come from a variety of sources, including scripture. We have also mentioned the fact that religious bookstores now offer us a choice of a huge array of resources. Whatever texts we use, readings and reflections are not hurried elements of prayer. They need to be slowly and carefully read, with plenty of time for pauses.

Movement/Gesture

Depending on the content and context of the payer, the group may be invited to do such things as light a candle, pick up and hold one of the symbols from the sacred space, share a sign of peace or stand. Part of the prayer preparation is deciding if and how the element of movement/gesture will be included.

Quiet Time/Silence

Silence is something with which many of us feel uncomfortable. However, it is a very necessary element within prayer. In fact, without silence our prayer is weakened. If we have no silence how will we hear God speaking to us?

Because the leader may feel a sense of responsibility for the group's prayer, he/she may in fact be more uncomfortable with silence than other members of the group. The silence may feel longer or more tension-filled than it actually is. The leader may sense restlessness within the group that in reality is not there. As a prayer leader, the leader should try to grow more and more comfortable with silence where it is appropriate and not rush along too quickly.

Shared Prayer/Reflections

This is another element of prayer that may be new and fearful for some members of the group. Nobody should ever feel that they have to share either a prayer or their own reflections on what has been read or experienced in the prayer. Such sharing should come freely from members.

When leading the prayer and inviting any sharing from the group, it is important to do so in a non-threatening manner. Do not be discouraged if people are slow to share their prayer/reflections. As time goes on the group will do so more readily.

Often a leader will find that there may be a significant silence before the first person shares a prayer/reflection. Then a number of other people may share quite quickly. The prayer leader needs to be patient during this initial silence and to resist the temptation to move on to the next element of prayer. When another significant silence emerges from the group it may then be time to move on.

Some prayer texts have specific intercessions within them and these may be ample for some prayer sessions.

Intercessions

When provided, the intercessions normally have a response for the group. The prayer leader may choose to lead these intercessions or to delegate a member of the group to do so.

Concluding Prayer

The leader can say the concluding prayer. Alternatively he/she might invite everybody to join in saying it together. If the prayer has begun with a sign of the cross, the leader invites people to bring it to a close with the same gesture.

Step Two: Select a text for the prayer

The next step is to select a text for the prayer. When doing this, it is helpful to reflect on the group who will be praying together. Perhaps there is a particular theme that would be good for the group to explore at this time. The theme might also be decided upon in light of the season in nature or in the church year. Again, there are many resources available. Many groups adopt a lectionary-based approach to prayer by building their prayer around the following Sunday's scripture readings. Resource 9.6 provides two sample texts that can be explored using the guidelines in the following section.

Step Three: Work with the text

As has been said, choosing the text is just the beginning of the preparation! The next step is to carefully read the text and enter into it. The questions in Resource 9.5 are designed as a guide to help those preparing and leading the prayer to engage in such a process of entering in.

It may be useful for the leader to photocopy these questions and use them as a work sheet for his/her preparation.

Once these questions have been explored, the leader will have a better sense of the spirit of the prayer while also knowing what practical preparations are needed for it.

Step Four: Use the following checklist for the final stage of preparation
Arrive early to allow plenty of time to set up.
Attend to the setting, making sure that the lighting, heating and seating arrangement will enhance rather than impede group prayer.
Create the sacred space.
If using taped music, have the music set and check that the machine works!
Delegate the tasks within the prayer to other members of the group.
Distribute the prayer sheets to the group and introduce the prayer.
Once the prayer begins, trust and let go. And let the Spirit work!

RESOURCE 9.5
GUIDING QUESTIONS FOR EXPLORING SELECTED PRAYER TEXTS

This resource is intended for on-going use within the leadership group. We anticipate that those responsible for preparing prayer for a leadership group meeting would use this resource to help them, once they have selected their text(s) for prayer.

1. What is the mood and message of the prayer?

2. What images do you find in the text?

3. What symbols suggest themselves for the sacred space (fabrics, colours, oils, incense, icons, branches, rocks, etc.)?

4. Is there any piece of music that the text suggests?

5. Are there any particular gestures or movements/actions that might form part of the prayer experience?

6. What tasks (e.g. readings, sections of reading) are there to delegate to others in the group, so as to maximise participation?

7. What will you say by way of introducing the prayer and focusing people at the beginning?

8. Where will there be pauses for silence?

9. Will you tell the readers when to begin or will they decide themselves?

10. If there is to be a concluding prayer at the end of the meeting, will you use some element from this text?

11. Will every one have a copy of the prayer?

RESOURCE 9.6 TWO SAMPLE PRAYER TEXTS

Below you will find two models of prayer texts that a leadership group might use. The first is based on a task of a parish leadership group (i.e. mission), the second is based on a seasonal theme (Easter). We have used the New Revised Standard Version as the source for the scripture texts.

PEOPLE OF LIGHT

Focusing
I have set you to be a light
for the nations;
so that you may bring salvation
to the ends of the earth. (Acts 13:47)

Scripture

You are the light of the world. A city built on a hill cannot be hid. No one after lighting a lamp puts it under the bushel basket, but on the lamp stand, and it gives light to all in the house. In the same way, let your light shine before others, so that they may see your good works and give glory to your Father in heaven. (Matthew 5:14-16)

Reflection
A Christian community is evangelised in order to evangelise.
A light is lit in order to give light.
A candle is not lit to be put under a basket, said Christ.
It's lit and put up high, in order to give light.
That is what a true community is like.

A community is a group of men and women who have found the truth
In Christ and in his gospel,
And who follow the truth and join together to follow it more strongly.
It is not just an individual conversion.
It is a family who believes, a group that accepts God.

In the group, each one finds that the brother or sister is a source of strength
And that, in moments of weakness, they help one another

And by loving one another and believing,
They give light and example.

The preacher no longer needs to preach,
For there are Christians who preach by their own lives.
(Oscar Romero, October 29, 1978)

Quiet time

Intercessions

Response: May we be people of light.

Creator God, you have made us as your people, called to proclaim your Good news to the world. R.

Loving Father, you have gifted us with a sense of your presence in our lives and missioned us to share this presence with others. R.

Through your Son, you have shown us the ways of light and truth in the world. R.

With the Spirit, you provide us with all we need to bring your message to others through the witness we give in our lives. R.

Concluding Prayer

All glory, honour and praise to the Father
All glory, honour and praise to the Son,
All glory, honour and praise to the Spirit
All living in us as One.

Be with us as we journey together
Be with us as we discover your way
Be with us as the light shining through us
Be with us now and each day.

RESTING IN THE WONDER OF EASTER

Focusing

Easter morn has come,
And its wonder rests deeply in our hearts.
For he has risen,
God's Word has spoken.
And this bright day dawning
Draws us into its glory.
Christ's people know the feast of new life.

Scripture

After the Sabbath, as the first day of the week was dawning, Mary Magdalene and the other Mary went to see the tomb. And suddenly there was a great earthquake; for an angel of the Lord, descending from heaven, came and rolled back the stone and sat on it. His appearance was like lightning, and his clothing white as snow. For fear of him the guards shook and became like dead men. But the angel said to the women, 'Do not be afraid; I know that you are looking for Jesus who was crucified. He is not here; for he has been raised, as he said. Come, see the place where he lay. Then go quickly and tell his disciples, 'He has been raised from the dead and indeed he is going ahead of you to Galilee; there you will see him.' This is my message for you.'

So they left the tomb quickly with fear and great joy, and ran to tell his disciples. (Matthew 28:1-8)

Psalm

I will give thanks to the Lord
with my whole heart;
I will tell of all your wonderful deeds. (Psalm 9:1)

Quiet reflection time

In the stillness we wait and pray – recounting and giving thanks for the wonder of resurrection promised us in the Easter experience.

Concluding Prayer

Glory to you Lord who calls us to resurrection,
Glory to you Lord who renews our lives through the Easter story.
Glory to you Lord whose power working in us can do more than we can
infinitely imagine. Amen.

SECTION TEN

Mission: Sustaining Parish Renewal

Introduction

Throughout this book we have concentrated on encouraging, supporting and resourcing collaborative parish leadership. We have, by necessity, focused on a very small group of parishioners and their priests. This focus is not meant to distract us from the wider issues. Rather we believe that if a parish leadership group is well prepared and working together then it is better able to confront the many challenges facing parish life today.

In terms of the many issues facing parish today, we believe that the issue of mission is emerging more and more as a central one. It is an issue that will require our attention into the future.

In the context of Parish Development and Renewal we are beginning to identify several strands of meaning when we talk about 'mission'. There is a 'from maintenance to mission' understanding – captured in a movement away from seeing parish as a centre of administration to seeing parish as the place where people live out their mission to be Christians in the world. This understanding invites the leadership group to support parishioners in living out this mission instead of directing their energy into maintaining parish structures that may no longer be serving an appropriate purpose. It necessitates communication, planning and strategic use of available resources.

Alongside this understanding we see two particular dynamics emerging when parishes begin to look at the area of mission – the dynamics of mission as outreach, and mission as evangelisation. These two dynamics are different from one another, primarily in that evangelisation suggests a more overt sharing of the gospel message. When a parish carries out a visitation it may be an exercise in outreach, but it is not always an exercise in evangelisation.

As an emerging issue for parishes today we recognise the infancy of the following resource material. However, in this initial stage of our exploration, we think it necessary to highlight the importance of the topic. We believe, also, that the following reflections can serve as a basis for a leadership group's own reflection and our continued learning.

At the end of this final section we develop the theme of mission into two practical expressions: Parish Visitation and Parish Clustering. The book is concluded with a resource on the virtue of hope.

RESOURCE 10.1 WHO IS PARISH RENEWAL FOR?

The following resource helps members of a parish leadership group to think in terms of all the members of the parish community. We suggest that the members read the reflection and use the questions at the end to help them in their discussion.

One cannot talk of mission without talking of context. The context for you as a leadership group is parish. We began this resource book by addressing the questions: What is a parish? And what is the context for renewal today? Here we need to look at who is the parish and, more specifically, who is parish renewal for?

We can say that parish renewal is for 100% of the parish

This statement is perhaps most helpfully considered in the light of 'belonging'. The common denominator for a sense of belonging in parish is not the level of active participation an individual has in the community but rather how much they feel part of the community.

Parish is made up of lay people, priests and vowed religious. Of these:
   # Some are involved in the leadership group and other groups and committees in the parish.
   # Some give of time and of themselves in liturgical ministries and some care for the church building and furnishings.
   # Some feel a sense of belonging but, because of their particular stage of life, find it difficult to be actively involved.
   # Some attend Mass and other services and may or may not have any sense of belonging. The same could be said of those who only attend Mass a few times a year.
   # Then there are those who live in the parish but feel alienated from the church and do not participate. Their belonging is perhaps based on feelings of hurt or injustice. They wish to belong but perhaps do not feel themselves welcome.
   # Then there are those who feel no sense of belonging and for whom parish has no relevance and they would express no need for belonging to parish, although they may acknowledge spiritual need.

Given all the above, we restate the belief that parish renewal is for 100% of the parish. Even given the fact that not all members in the geographical setting of the parish will be Catholic, or even Christian, we can still aspire to renewal impacting all the community, and to every member of the community having something to contribute to that renewal.

Discussion Questions
    Does the above reflect your experience of your parish?
    What are the similarities?
    What are the differences?
    Do you agree that parish renewal is for 100% of the parish?
    In light of the above understanding and your own parish situation, what do you see as the challenges facing your parish in the near future?
    Does this have any practical implications for you as a leadership group in the parish?

RESOURCE 10.2 MISSION: THE VOCATION OF ALL CHRISTIANS

The following passage is taken from *Christifideles Laici,* par 14. It offers some insights into the church's understanding of the mission of the laity. We suggest that it would be very helpful for group members to read through and reflect on this material together. It could be incorporated into the prayer time given within a leadership group's meeting. We have concluded the passage with some reflection questions that may help facilitate discussion within the group.

At the heart of the vocation of all Christians is mission

The living tradition of the church has always recognised that the baptised share in Christ's mission of prophet, priest and king. In the wake of Vatican II, Pope John Paul set out to emphasise this truth.

He who was born of the Virgin Mary, he said, 'has come to make us into a kingdom of priests'. Vatican II reminds us that the mission of Christ – priest, prophet/teacher and king – continues in the church and is shared by the whole people of God.

Pope John Paul urges the laity to absorb the rich teachings of Vatican II on their sharing of Christ's mission. Basically what it teaches is this:

The laity share in Christ's priestly mission
Incorporated into him
They share in his sacrifice on the cross
When they offer themselves
and their work to God.
All their daily work and prayer,
their family life and leisure,
their hardships and difficulties too,
become sacrifices offered in the eucharist
with Christ's sacrifice.
Thus, by their daily life and actions
The laity consecrate the world itself to God.

The laity share in Christ's mission
as Prophet-Teacher.
This gives them the capacity
to believe the gospel
and the responsibility
to proclaim it with courage.
They come to appreciate the church's faith
that cannot err in matters of belief.
They are called to allow the gospel's power
to shine out in their everyday lives.
Despite all contemporary contradictions
They must proclaim their hope
of future glory.

The laity share Christ's priestly mission

And he calls them to spread the kingdom.
How do they show this kingship?
Chiefly by their efforts to overcome
the kingdom of evil within themselves.
Then by their service of Christ who is present
in all his sisters and brothers,
they are called to restore to the created world all its original value.
Doing this they share the power of Christ
who subjects all creation and himself
to the Father so that God
may be everything to everyone (Cor 15:28)

This sharing in Christ's threefold mission
is begun in baptism,
developed in confirmation
and realised in eucharist.
It is given to each one individually
because each individually
is one of the many
who form the one Body of Christ.

This sharing
Which springs from church communion
Must be lived in communion
And for the deepening of that communion.
(*Christifideles Laici* 14, from *This is the Laity,* Grail Publications, 1989)

Reflection questions
    What does this passage say to you?
    What challenges does it present to you as a leadership group?
    How can you as a leadership group support people in hearing and acting upon its message?

RESOURCE 10.3: MISSION, NOT SERVICE

This resource is intended to help members of a leadership group take on board the contemporary understanding of mission, acknowledging the past models that have influenced us. Again we suggest that the group read the material below and honestly share on the reflection questions that follow.

Toward a new understanding of mission

Mission can have particular associations for people. Amongst these are:
  • An over association of mission with religious and clergy overseas
  • An over dependence on a vision of mission as service 'to' rather that 'with' people.

There is a lot of talk about the parish today being mission territory, evangelising territory. There can be a sense, at times, that behind this notion is an attitude that regards mission as service and suggests that God is absent in 'mission territory'. This service model would tell us to get out there and bring God to this territory; however a truly missionary model would tell us to get out there and meet God.

Before the Second Vatican Council the notion of mission was firmly associated with the 'missionaries' who worked in foreign countries. The notion of mission was also very closely associated with 'service'. However, since the Council and the 1987 Synod it has become more clearly re-focused. All are called to mission, all laymen and laywomen are to live out their discipleship and mission through their callings in life.

One of the reasons we find it difficult to move from an understanding of mission as 'overseas' to mission as an intrinsic baptismal call, is that mission has become very tied up with our idea of service. Yet:
  # Service is something I do *for* other people
  # Mission is what I do *with and alongside* other people.

These are two very different models. The ability to see the difference is an important step for any group on the way to adopting a missionary mindset.

When a parish group looks to its mission it can be difficult to discover a real missionary spirituality amidst a prevailing attitude of service. Mission includes but is not service. At the heart of mission is a spirituality, a spiritual attitude. That attitude tells us that God is there; God is in all the situations, places, and people of the parish. We do not take God to people, rather we go and find, connect with and hopefully communicate with God – our God who is already present.

Reflection questions

What do you think the difference is between a service and a missionary mindset?

Can you think of any practical examples as to how these differences might be seen in a parish setting?

Does this have any implications for our work together as a parish leadership group?

RESOURCE 10.4 MISSION AS DIALOGUE

In the introduction to this section we noted the importance of communication in the context of mission. The following resource helps to underscore this, viewing real dialogue as a key element of mission. The resource is followed by questions that help place reflection in the context of the life and work of the parish leadership group.

Exploring the notion of dialogue

Understanding mission as dialogue is described by Donal Dorr[3] as a corrective to the older notions of mission. This new understanding of mission, the notion of mission as dialogue, '... conveys the impression that mission is not just a matter of doing things for people. It is first of all a matter of being with people, of listening and sharing with them'.

Further, in the parish context, it is important to remember that dialogue, as opposed to listening, is two-way. Beginning with ourselves, it means that we have to be willing to reveal ourselves and our beliefs. It is important that we are honest about who we are and what we believe. This is a challenge to all involved in parish life, for clergy, leadership, those in ministries and all parishioners.

So, on the one hand, we believe that we have something valuable to offer, the good news. On the other hand, dialogue is not about trying to persuade people of our position but to be open and attentive to what people are telling us about their experience, values as well as concerns. This is the two-way nature of true dialogue.

A real question we need to ask in parish today is, 'Are we prepared to be influenced by dialogue?' This may seem a strange question but as church we are very used to people coming to us on our terms. We are less used to being open to real influence and, ultimately, change.

Questions for the parish leadership group

As a parish leadership group:

> With whom should you be dialoguing at this time and in the near future?

---

3. *Mission Today,* Donal Dorr, Columba Press, 2000.

What strategies can you employ to engage in real dialogue in your parish?

How will you prepare yourselves to hear what people have to say – including what you would rather not hear?

What help will you need before, during and after such dialogue?

RESOURCE 10.5

OUTREACH AND EVANGELISATION:

COMING TO A DEEPER UNDERSTANDING OF MISSION

The following resource will help parish leadership groups to come to an understanding of the difference between outreach and evangelisation. It will also surface basic questions that we believe any group addressing the issue of missions should ask of itself. These questions are interspersed as headings in the text. We suggest that the group discuss the material and the questions contained within it together.

Asking the questions

As we said in our introduction to this section, outreach and evangelisation are aspects of the dynamic of mission. It seems that, more and more the choice to be Christian will be exactly that, a choice. Because of this there is perhaps a need to be less self-conscious when talking about witness to the world and a need to be more missionary at home than we might have been in previous generations. For parish groups intent on outreach and/or evangelisation it may be helpful to examine what exactly we mean by the terms in order to help us to discern what we are about.

Further to this first step it may be useful to look at the following questions: What are we about? From what do we reach out? What do we offer? Into what do we invite people? And finally, what are our hopes for the future?

What are we about?

In terms of what we are about, we suggest that outreach and evangelisation are not the same.

Outreach may seek to welcome new people into the geographical area of the parish. There may be focused outreach to particular groups in the parish – youth, elderly, young mothers.

Outreach may seek to contact and dialogue with those who feel alienated or marginalised.

Outreach may seek to identify and respond to particular social needs in the community in the name of the parish.

The above descriptions of outreach do not necessarily preclude evangelisation but it seems to us that evangelisation is something quite specific and something quite new for Irish parishes.

Evangelisation at its heart is about presenting the good news of Christ clearly, through our words and our actions, so that those who hear and see are drawn to commit themselves completely to Christ and to his church. It will often involve re-presenting the good news of Christ to those who have heard it before. It will involve the necessary starting point of openness to our own re-evangelisation or self-evangelisation. We ourselves need to know what we believe, as well as why.

You may feel neither familiar nor particularly comfortable with this language or the associated images. In our work with parish groups we hear a lot about people's genuine desire to make the parish a living witness to God's love for God's people. We suggest that to be an evangelising parish we may need to re-look at our starting point. We may need to ask firstly how we make ourselves living witnesses to God's love for God's people.

From what do we reach out?

Thus, the initial answer we would give to the above question is 'myself'. When we question what we reach out from and recognise it as within ourselves, then we are more inclined to see the need for a self-evangelisation. What do we believe? Why do we believe? What are we called to? We don't simply dive into the task of reaching out to others. We begin with ourselves and an openness to re-hearing the Christian message. Then we might be ready to respond to the gospel imperative to 'go and preach'.

What do we offer?

The responses to our baptism and to the gospel missionary imperative will be carried out in different ways in each parish community. This may provide an insight into our role as evangelisers but perhaps the next question focuses us more. We can answer it by saying that what we seek to offer, in the light of the gospel, is fullness of life.

A word of caution: A necessary awareness to carry with us is this – very often those to whom we think we are offering something are actually the ones doing the giving! It is helpful to be willing and ready to graciously embrace the evangelisation that others will carry out in us.

In each parish, when we work towards visitation, assemblies, surveys and other models for evangelisation, how do we answer this question of what do we offer?

Into what do we invite people?

In terms of our local parish community we can usefully ask what do we invite people into? We can say we invite people into a community of believers, a church, but what does that look like in your parish? If in response to your evangelisation I come along to the parish church for a liturgy or a meeting, what will I see? What will I experience? What does the invitation to fullness of life look like in your parish?

What are our hopes for the future?

Finally, in answer to 'what do we hope for the future?', we hope that we will experience having life and having it to the full because we believe that this is what has been offered to us. What does the experience of 'life to the full' look like in your parish? How is this expressed in the way we are and what we do?

Group discussion

 As a group, discuss the material using the headings as questions for the group.

 Use the group's discussion on this material and the material from the previous resources in this section as ground work for the practical exercise in resource 10.6

RESOURCE 10.6 TOWARDS A COMMON UNDERSTANDING OF MISSION

The term 'mission', as we have been using it in this section, carries with it a particular meaning that may be new for many people. This newness calls for some reflection on our behalf on how we approach the topic of mission in our parishes.

This is because the lens we employ when we look at 'mission' has a very definite bearing on how we take up the invitation to be a missionary people. If we view mission as bringing God to people, or as *doing for* others, our starting point will be different from those who view mission as acknowledging the God already present, and mission as *doing with* others. These different understandings will affect significantly the choices parish leadership groups make regarding adopting a missionary mindset in the parish context.

We believe, therefore, that embracing the call to mission can be helped by a conscious acknowledgement of and grappling with our own starting point *vis-à-vis* mission. To this end, the following exercise is offered to facilitate a leadership group's articulation of its understanding of mission – an understanding that we believe will ultimately affect how the group functions in the parish.

This resource is followed by a resource that will help the group adopt agreed-upon characteristics of a missionary mindset that will impact how it works. These two resources are, therefore, closely related and so are recommended to be done in tandem.

Note: This is an example of a resource that we feel would benefit from outside facilitation.

Coming to a common understanding of mission

The following outline is one model of how a leadership group might share and come to a common understanding of mission.

Members of the leadership group read resource material 10.1-10.5 and the introduction to this resource as groundwork for carrying out this exercise.

The group decides to give significant time during its meeting to sharing and coming to a common understanding of mission. (This time might be spread over a couple of meetings or it might be decided to give time outside of the normal group meetings to do this exercise.)

The prayer at the beginning of the meeting has a mission focus. (See the resource sample in section 9.)

Individual members are given time to answer the following reflection questions by themselves. Background music might be played while they do this. Pens and paper are available for those who want to write out their thoughts.

When people are ready, members share their reflection within the group, with whoever is facilitating noting divergences and convergences of thought.

The group then moves on to the next resource, exploring together the hallmarks of a missionary mindset. (Both these resources might be done in one session or spread out over two, depending on the group's and the facilitator's preference.)

Reflection questions

When I think of the term 'mission' what immediately comes to mind?
From my reading and reflection on this section of the resourcebook, has my understanding of mission changed?
What do I think mission means now?
What bearing might this meaning have for the work of this leadership group?

RESOURCE 10.7 THE HALLMARKS OF A MISSIONARY MINDSET

This resource identifies what we consider to be central hallmarks of a missionary mindset. They are not given in order of priority. As will be seen, each of them has a very definite practical bearing on how a leadership group might take on board a missionary mindset in the parish.

The facilitator can decide how best to work through this material. For example, the headings might be written up on chart paper and addressed in that way. These notes are concluded by questions to help members respond to the information.

Communication

In the context of mission, communication assumes an openness and transparency on the part of all involved. In mission there are no hidden agendas, no secret strategies, no ulterior motives. To this end, communication is about being honest and open in our approaches, about what we are doing and about why we are doing it. Communication is, of necessity, two-way. We need to be conscious that communication associated with our work is not only coming from one direction.

Listening

If in mission we are *doing with* others, then we have to be prepared to engage in real listening. This means that we have to listen to the people with whom we wish to be engaged in mission, to be able to hear their voices and to be willing to hear what those voices are saying – words which we may not always like! And hearing means being open to being changed in the process.

Discernment

This reminds us that we do not go into action with all the answers in our back pocket. It also reminds us that finding the way forward is not caught up solely in analysis or good strategies. Discernment is a listening to the call of the Spirit in our hearts and in the world. Where is God calling us to action? What are the signs of the Spirit in our midst? Where are those signs leading us?

Prayer

Discernment cannot take place without making a conscious space for prayer. Our encounter with God in prayer reminds us of the wonder of our call to share in the work of God in building the kingdom. It focuses us on the purpose of all we do and it nourishes us with the strength to go forward together.

Planning

Prayer and discernment do not let us off the hook of planning. Responsibly listening to the Spirit through discerning prayer calls for a response on our part. We cannot sit back and say that God will do it for us. The whole point is that we are given the privilege of sharing in God's plan for us, that we are called into partnership. It makes sense then that, as responsible partners in our relationship with God, we will look to the future and be proactive. We can try to discern future needs and directions for the parish. We can plan for the next 1, 3, 5 years for our parish. Not only can we – we should!

On-going formation

Embracing a missionary mindset launches us on a journey of discovery, into new ways and new insights. Along the way we will realise that we need new tools to help us on the journey. As we work with people, the truth of their voice calls us to new places and to new understandings. Perhaps what we knew in the past will not help us in the present. Perhaps the situations in which we find ourselves call for new learning, new responses.

All this points to the reality that in our individual and collective journeys to God we are always changing and being changed. If we wish to continue this journey fruitfully, then openness to on-going formation is a necessity.

A parish leadership group needs to be concerned with on-going formation in two spheres. On-going formation for itself, as new discoveries, tasks and responses emerge in its work. And on-going formation for the wider parish as its members move forward together and strive to be a vibrant Christian community in the context of the reality of their lives.

Recognition of mutual dignity

In a missionary mindset, our starting point is the mutual dignity of the people of God – an equality exemplified in baptism. It is this starting point that will help us make the move from doing 'for' to doing 'with' people. Imagine what it would mean in our communities if we were to look at all its members and affirm their dignity and equality – no matter the gender, perceived social status, race, age ... It is this understanding that will go towards helping each of us claim our identity as 'adults' in the church, called and empowered to play our part.

Discussion questions

How do you consider the above hallmarks?

What would you add to the list? Why?

What practical bearing do/could these hallmarks have on how we go about our work in this leadership group?

The facilitator should record the discussion from the above before moving onto the final stage of this resource.

Consensus

From the findings in Resource 10.6 and the questions above, the leadership group try to come to some consensus on:

A common understanding of mission.

The characteristic hallmarks they wish to adopt that will be reflected in how they go about mission in the parish.

RESOURCE 10.8 A PRACTICAL EXPRESSION OF MISSION: PARISH VISITATION

In the light of the current situation, and with a real sense of mission, we need to create opportunities for dialogue. One way that is being tried by parishes is through visitation. This is not a new pastoral practice but it is one that is being revisited and revamped in the light of current challenges. One of the biggest changes from the past practice of parish visitation is that now and in the future visitation is more likely to be carried out by lay people along with their priests rather than by priests alone. The following draws on the experience of parishes that have discerned, planned for and carried out a visitation programme.

The information within this resource covers the following areas:
Why parish visitation?
What is needed for effective visitation?
Where do we start?
The visitation team
Long-term planning (post-visitation)
Formation for a visitation team
The commissioning of a visitation team

Why parish visitation?

A sense of belonging is a hallmark of a Christian community and therefore of a parish. In our present pastoral situation, outreach is a particular concern and one that is part of the mission and vocation of all Christians. It is one way a parish community can show that it is caring for itself. Most parishes are concerned about reaching out to those who are no longer in contact with the church. Setting up a parish visitation team is a way of maintaining a connection with those who are part of the parish and renewing contact with those who may feel alienated.

What is needed for effective parish visitation

To be effective a visitation programme requires *commitment* and *prayer*:
• It requires that the fulltime parish team and the leadership group be interested in and committed to the concept, the work, the consequences and the long-term planning that comes with parish visitation.

- It requires that prayer be central to parish visitation. This requirement is also an ideal way to involve the whole parish. Some who are involved in the visitation will pray together. Other parishioners may pray at home or in church while the visitation is actually taking place.

Where do we start?

Once there is a commitment to parish visitation on the part of the fulltime parish team, it is important to open out the idea to the parish leadership group. It is important to explore the following questions:

Why are we engaging in a parish visitation?

On whose authority are parishioners visiting the homes?

How might it best be done in our situation?

When will it be done – time of year, day, hour?

Who will do it – age profile, gender, lay, religious, cleric?

What areas would be visited, and in what order?

What would be the follow-up from a visitation?

What formation would be required and who would give it to those involved in visitation?

The visitation team

The leadership group, possibly in consultation with other groups in the parish, need to discuss and decide how to go about getting a visitation team. It will need to look at identifying suitable people to form the team. Identifying suitable people is vital since not all parishioners have the skills/gifts for this ministry. Some of the gifts/skills required include people with a sense of the parish, of the Christian community, social skills, ability to work with others, an openness and willingness to really listen to others, and commitment. Once a team of people has been gathered, a process of formation has to be undertaken.

Long-term planning (Post-visitation)

Some parishes see the visitation as an end in itself, with no need for further follow up. Other parishes see the visitation as the first step towards possible parish gatherings, e.g. retreats, missions and other forms of renewal.

Parish visitation may also lead to a parish listening survey to further the needs of the parishioners. After the visitation there may be a gathering of the people visited in a collection of houses/roads or one estate. A number of smaller gatherings may then lead to a parish assembly the following year.

Formation for visitation teams

There are many benefits to be gained by having a formation course for a parish visitation team.

- It serves as a bonding experience for the team, giving them time to develop mutual support and encouragement.
- Through the content of the course the visitors are more likely to face into their task with an appropriate disposition.
- A formation course gives the participants the confidence to go about their allocated task. They will have a better understanding of what they are doing, why they are doing it and how best to go about it.
- By going through the course they are more likely to embrace this ministry with enthusiasm.

A formation course for a visitation team might include a focus on the following:

- The call of the gospel, i.e. the sending out of the seventy two disciples.
- Reasons for the visitation. It is important to have unity among the group as to why the visitation is taking place.
- Input, information and clarification on the parish/parishioners. The different areas and the traditions that go with each. A visitation team may decide to visit certain sections of the parish over a period of time. It is best to start small and cover one area at a time.
- Fears and expectations of those who would do the visitation. For many this will be their first experience of 'knocking on doors'.
- Partnership. As people will be calling in pairs, who goes with whom? Some people work well together and give each other energy for the visitation.
- Timing of the visitation. It is best that it takes place at the same time every week, e.g. 8:00-9:00 p.m. on a Wednesday. This is for the sake of the team and for the parishioners who know when to expect a visit.
- 'What do we say when we get to the door' If asked a question, will we be able to answer? It is good to do some role play as part of the training for the visitation.

- Listening exercises – there are skills that we can acquire to help us to be better listeners.
- What do we take with us, if anything? It is a helpful introduction to have a parish card, and or prayer card or parish calendar when on visitation. It is also important to remember that the team are going as witnesses to the good news, not as sales people!
- Advertising the visitation. If there is some publicity prior to visitation in the local papers, parish newsletter, notices at Mass, etc., it can give an added energy to the process. It is also good to keep parishioners informed on the progress of the visitation.
- Review and evaluation procedures both during and after the visitation. It is important that the team share what has happened in a spirit of prayer. Some groups meet directly after the visitation. This is not always convenient since some may be finished before others. Each group has to work out the time that is best for them.
- Commissioning of the visitation team. Once the training has been complete then it is important that there is a formal sending out of the team to the parish.
- Prayer should begin each formation session.

Commissioning of the visitation team

Ideally the commissioning ceremony takes place after the homily at the Sunday eucharist. In this case, the readings of the day will be part of the commissioning. However, it is not always possible to have the commissioning at a weekend Mass. A ceremony could take place at the end of the training sessions for the visitation team.

The following is a model of the steps a ceremony might take – it will need to be adapted or rearranged to suit your team.

Opening Hymn
Greeting and Welcome
Readings
Reflection (Another reading that is not scripture based, a piece of writing or poetry might seem appropriate at this stage. This might also take the form of gesture, mime or dance.)

Commissioning: (Model)

Parish Priest: For some time now you have been preparing to be a member of this visitation team. Do you understand the special role that you have in carrying out this mission?

Team Members: Yes

Parish Priest: Do you agree to use your gifts and talents to promote God's work in this task?

Team Members: Yes

Giving of appropriate symbol (e.g. prayer candle, an angel on my shoulder or some other symbol decided by the individual parish).

Parish Priest: N, you have been called to the ministry of visitation. I send you out as a representative of this parish.

Intercessions
Closing Prayer
Closing Hymn

RESOURCE 10.9: A PRACTICAL EXPRESSION OF MISSION:
PARISH CLUSTERING

This resource explains the practical notion of clustering – a strategy increasingly employed at local parish level.

We suggest that a leadership group first read through the material in this resource and then explore the questions at the end together.

What is clustering?

Essentially clustering happens when particular groups commit to working together towards a common purpose. Groups may come together around particular events, issues, concerns or on-going activities.

This practice has been present in the secular world for some time. We probably all know of community or support groups with similar aspirations and tasks who cluster together for the purpose of mutual support, encouragement and the sharing of resources. When groups are small, resources limited and concerns common, it makes sense to work together with others.

Clustering in a Christian context

More and more we are hearing about clustering at parish level, within deaneries and at diocesan level. In a Christian context clustering brings with it an extra dimension, beyond a utilitarian benefit. The difference lies in the purpose and the manner in which the practice of clustering is undertaken.

Purpose

In chapter four of the letter to the Ephesians we find a clear reminder to us of the reason for the gifts with which we have been graced. All these gifts have been given '... to knit God's holy people together for the work of service to build up the Body of Christ.' (v. 12a)

This quotation carries with it many reminders to us:
  • It brings us right back to our understanding of mission. The mission of each of us is to bring about the kingdom of God.
  • It reminds us that we carry out this mission together. We are not mavericks or solo artists; we are members of the Body of Christ. This body is called to work as one living, vibrant unit.

• It alerts us to the reality that a gift is not something to be possessed. It is something to be shared. Its purpose only makes sense when it is put to use – for the service of our mission.

• It reminds us that the church is bigger than our parish. There always exists the temptation to get very insular in our outlook. The possibility of clustering gives us a very concrete opportunity to connect with the reality of the church of the diocese, as well as of the parish.

In clustering, a group of parishes sets goals for themselves that will enable them together to build up the Body of Christ in a particular way. In this way the resources and gifts that have been given to them individually can be utilised for the wider good.

Process

The purpose of clustering in a Christian context is mission-centred. It makes sense, then, to ground any decisions about how, where and when to cluster, in prayer. It is the power of the Holy Spirit working through us that will help us discern the way forward and empower us to complete the work set before us.

Common purposes/tasks/goals

The concept of clustering might become clearer by looking to examples of clustering that have taken place in the recent past. The examples we are offering come from our experience within the Dublin Diocese.

Jubilee events: Many adjacent parishes came together to see what they could do jointly in the Jubilee year. This resulted in people attending events in other parishes and parishes sharing the same event, for example the national day of pilgrimage.

Fraternal homily preparation: A number of groups of priests around the diocese come together weekly to prepare their Sunday homilies. In some cases this is accompanied with a cup of tea and a chat. In other cases the preparation is followed by a shared lunch. In one deanery area, the priests were invited to meet in the Vicar Forane's house. Initially the purpose was to prepare homilies but there is an openness to see where it might go from there.

Training: Some parishes have chosen to cluster for the training of their leadership groups, baptism teams, liturgy groups etc. This has the added advantage of allowing for the sharing of any cost involved. But an even greater advantage is the support and goodwill shared among people from different parishes who are going through similar experiences.

Youth Workers: A number of parishes have clustered for the purpose of employing a youth worker for the area.

Common, pressing issues: Parishes have clustered around exploring parish responses to particular common concerns, i.e. drugs, youth, marriage break-down.

The Liturgical Year: Days on Advent, Lent and other liturgical seasons were shared by a number of parishes through out the diocese.

Looking to the future: Parishes that are close to one another have come together to look to the future needs of their area and to work on a common and cohesive vision for the future.

How often should a cluster group meet?

How often a cluster group will meet will be determined by the purpose of the cluster. For example, priests who meet to prepare their homilies will of necessity have to meet weekly. Other groups may decide to meet monthly, every few months or even annually – again depending on the purpose.

Who should meet?

If and when parishes decide to cluster with each other it is necessary to have the support of the relevant clergy involved. To this end the clergy of these parishes may find themselves meeting to discuss the practical possibilities and implications of clustering.

After that, those involved in the tasks and visioning associated with the purpose of the cluster, should be included in any cluster meetings.

What is involved?

Prayer and discernment: When a number of parishes come together to consider clustering they should make sure that adequate time is given to prayer and discernment around the direction they should take. This will help avoid rash decisions that may leave some parishes feeling railroaded or, down the road, other parishes with a sense that they have wasted their time.

A common goal: It is vital for the cluster to articulate a very definite and precise common goal for itself. This will help ensure that all involved fully understand the purpose of the cluster. It will also help ensure that some parishes do not have unrealistic expectations of the work of the cluster. The goal is something that they can achieve together and is something around which all involved have energy.

Set procedures and parameters: All involved should be clear and in agreement about how the goal is going to be achieved. Questions such as the following need to be asked before the work of the cluster begins: Who is going to oversee the work? Who is going to carry out the work? How are any costs going to be shared? How are we going to keep open the lines of communication among us? What are the limits of this task? What do we consider acceptable and what is not?

Implementation: Obviously the cluster will need to implement its goal as efficiently as possible.

Review and future planning: When a particular cluster initiative is completed the experience should be reviewed. What helped the initiative? What could have been better? What have we learned? Was it a worthwhile experience? What next?

Group reflection questions

What do you see as the benefits of clustering?

What do you see as the drawbacks?

What are the possibilities for clustering that you see for your parish and those around you? (i.e. Are there particular issues, events, concerns around which it might be good to cluster with surrounding parishes?)

Are there other people in the parish you need to talk to about clustering?

Where do you go from here as regards the practice of clustering?

RESOURCE 10.10 CALLED TO BE PEOPLE OF HOPE

The Christian virtue of hope is a key aspect of our identity as Christians – an aspect that is often neglected but one we would be wise to address. This resource explores this virtue in the light of people's experience and the call of the church to be people of hope. It begins with a tool for personal reflection, moving on to a teasing out of the virtue of hope and concludes by helping the group to reflect on the implications of this for the group and its work.

Exploring our own experience

Each of us can point to times in our lives when we feel a sense of struggle, confusion, even despair. These feelings affect how we are in our selves and how we are with others. They affect our relationships, our attitude to life and how we go about things in our day-to-day existence.

Equally we can point to times when we feel very positive about life, to times when we feel full of hope and energy. These feelings, too, affect how we are in our selves and how we are with others. They affect our relationships, our attitude to life and how we go about things in our day-to-day existence.

We can learn a lot about the virtue of hope by reflecting on these different experiences within ourselves.

Reflection questions

1. As an individual think of a time in your life when you felt a sense of despair.
    How did it affect how you felt in general?
    How did it affect your relationship with others?
    How did it affect how you went about the tasks of your life at the time?
    Was there anything in particular that helped you to overcome these feelings of despair?

2. As the group feels free to do, members share on the above questions with the aim of drawing out an overall picture of the effects of despair and, in particular, how one might move from despair to a sense of hope. Record these findings within the group.

3. As an individual think of a time in your life when you felt a sense of hope.

How did it affect how you felt in general?

How did it affect your relationship with others?

How did it affect how you went about the tasks of your life at the time?

4. Again as the group feels free to do, share on the above questions. This time try to draw out an overall picture of the positive effects of having an attitude of hope. Again record the findings within the group.

Hope and the leadership group

Hope is a dimension of the soul and it is not essentially dependent on some particular observation of the world. It is an orientation of the spirit, an orientation of the heart. It is anchored somewhere beyond the world's horizons. Hope – in this deep and powerful sense – is not the same as joy that things are going well, but rather, an ability to work for something because it is good, not just because it stands a chance to succeed. It is hope, above all, which gives us the strength to live and continually try new things.' (Vacslav Havel)

As leaders within the parish it is very important that members of a leadership group approach their role in a spirit of hope. This spirit of hope is a Christian virtue to which each of us is called. It is a hope that will not disappoint us (Romans 5:5) because it is a hope founded in our belief in God.

In today's climate hope is an important topic for a leadership group to explore. As leaders within the parish, ideally group members will model for others a stance of hope to parish life. As was seen from the above reflection questions, if we carry with us this spirit of hope our responses in situations will be very different.

This is because hope and despair bring with them two very different stances and responses to life, and the situations that arise in life. In a spirit of despair we are apt to experience a paralysis that robs us of seeing possibilities or future directions. Our response will be one of surrender, a loss of energy, perhaps anger, confusion, frustration and often inaction.

A stance of hope, on the other hand, brings with it the ability to look at seemingly difficult situations with an eye for new possibilities, new responses, and new ways. There is a far greater likelihood that out of this stance people will find energy within to embrace difficult or unknown issues, rather than run away from them.

From the above it could be said that even outside of any Christian context, hope is, objectively, a good thing. But within the Christian context there is much to add. As Cardinal Henry Newman said, there is reason for the hope within – and that reason is the person of Jesus Christ and our share in his story through baptism.

As Christians, hope is constitutive of who we are. As people who share in the new life of resurrection in and through our baptism, we are made to be people of hope. This means that when confronted with particular life situations we are called to respond in a particular way – in a way of hope.

When we talk about hope we are not talking about a blind trust that something outside of ourselves will resolve a difficult or unknown situation. We are not called to sit back and trust that God will work it out for us. Hope calls us into partnership.

We see this partnership in the reality that the only presumption that hope makes is that God has given us the tools we need for our journey. A fundamental aspect of hope is the willingness on our part to discover the tools that God has already given us individually and collectively – and to use them.

Seeing the signs of hope

An important part of the work of a leadership group is being able to see the signs of hope around it. In the life of your parish what seeds of hope are growing?

    # What about the tremendous hope that can be seen in the work of baptism teams?

    # What about the increased level of listening that is taking place in parishes through parish assemblies, listening surveys and parish visitation?

    # What about how we have rediscovered the old way of pilgrimage in a new way?

    # What about the growing interest in adult formation, *lectio divina* and other prayer methods?

\# What about the new sense of responsibility that comes with a growing sense of choice around church membership?

There are many things about which to be hopeful – even some things that might seem negative at an initial glance. In a spirit of hope we are freed to think of creative responses, of new ways forward; we are not tied by the old and trusted ways that may no longer work in our particular situation.

Group reflection questions

What is your reaction to the above?

What do you see as signs of hope in your parish?

Can you name realities in your parish that need to be faced in a spirit of hope?

How does all the above affect the role of the leadership group in the parish and how you carry out that role in the future?

Conclusion

Throughout this book we have been presenting some pathways towards the parish of the future. These are based on the experience of parishes involved in the Parish Development and Renewal process in the Dublin Archdiocese.

As we look to the future, the importance of structures for participation and belonging is central. But these structures will only be relevant if the underlying mindset is focused on collaboration and if this collaboration is rooted in and directed outward from a gospel faith.

To this extent the future of parish renewal needs to be grounded as much in individual holiness and faithfulness as it does in good theory and practice. For it is from our faith in Jesus Christ that our commitment and our energy flows. And we can say with confidence that the work of renewal needs both in abundance!